GLAD IT'S OVER
Inside Crystal Palace 1997 - 1998

BY

DOMINIC FIFIELD

A Crystal Palace official publication

BARON
MCMXCVIII

PUBLISHED BY BARON BIRCH
FOR CRYSTAL PALACE FOOTBALL CLUB
AND PRODUCED BY MORETON PRESS

© Dominic Fifield

All rights reserved. No part of this publication may be reproduced, stored in a retrieval system, or transmitted, in any form or by any means, electronic, mechanical, photocopying, recording or otherwise, without the prior permission of Baron Books.

Any copy of this book issued by the Publisher as clothbound or as a paperback is sold subject to the condition that it shall not by way of trade or otherwise, be lent, re-sold, hired out or otherwise circulated without the Publisher's prior consent, in any form of binding or cover other than that in which it is published, and without a similar condition including this condition being imposed on a subsequent purchaser.

ISBN 0 86023 599 8

Contents

Acknowledgements 6
Foreword by Mark Goldberg 7

1 – May-June '97 Hip Hop Hooray! 9
2 – July-August Just one Lombardo 14
3 – September Mauled by the Tigers 21
4 – October-November Padovano... invested wisely 28
5 – December Zohar not so good 37
6 – January-February '98 Everyone thrashes them 45
7 – March ...Being run over by a lorry! 54
8 – April Goodbye and Good Riddance 63
9 – May-June '98 Thank God it's all over 72

Illustrations 79
Appendix i Palace Results 1997-1998 91
Appendix ii Premiership Table 1997-1998 92
Index 93

*A*CKNOWLEDGEMENTS

While writing this book, I have been most fortunate in the generosity of friends, family and work colleagues. Some have been good enough to read parts of the manuscript, contributing suggestions, interviews or information, especially my mother, Bev, Andy, Rob and Chris. Thanks also to Neil Witheroe, Rob Ellis, Wags and Paul Romain for their perspectives on last season. Thanks to Pete and James at Palace, and to the Club for supplying so much intrigue with which to work!

PICTURES OPPOSITE TITLE PAGE:
Selhurst Park, Mark Goldberg and Ron Noades.

FOREWORD

by Mark Goldberg, Chairman, Crystal Palace FC

The 1997/98 season was a painful one for players, management and supporters of Crystal Palace Football Club. With high expectations following promotion to the Premier League, the club was beset with injuries which decimated our squad and rendered a more than useful start to the campaign obsolete, particularly after Christmas when we suffered most of all and even lost our influential coach, Ray Lewington.

On a personal level, however, I was able to fulfil one of my lifetime ambitions in the summer of 1998. Following a long, drawn-out process, I took charge of Crystal Palace Football Club in June, succeeding Ron Noades as chairman of the Club I have supported through thick and thin for years. Any supporter can imagine my joy at achieving such a goal. I have been a dedicated fan since my childhood in local Bromley and, when I realised that my own footballing skills would not forge me a career in the professional game, I set myself the target of becoming involved in some capacity at my beloved Selhurst Park. Years of hard work in the business world have allowed me to achieve this.

Inevitably, the takeover from Ron Noades was a complicated deal which involved a certain amount of leeway on both sides of the table. Such multi-million pound deals invariably throw up unforeseen problems and the deal on which we ultimately agreed was far removed from any agreement we had envisaged last October. While there were times when I doubted that the takeover would go through, I was intent on succeeding and have now secured the Club I love.

I am a 'football man' through and through. I was a keen player in my time, although I was not blessed with the skill of a Wright or Lombardo (!), and enjoyed a spell as manager of Beckenham Town. While I still turn out in the odd charity game, my influence is probably best reserved as Chairman of the Eagles as we enter a new, exciting era at Crystal Palace.

The on-the-field events of 1997/98 were bitterly disappointing. We have to learn from them in order to avoid similar failings ever occurring again. Crystal Palace has the potential to become one of the biggest clubs in this country, boasting a huge catchment area and a passionate support. I am convinced that we can achieve great things here in South London and, in so doing, banish the memories of last season.

Dominic Fifield's book gives a fascinating insight into events at the Club over the unsuccessful Premiership campaign. It certainly was an extraordinary season — multi-million pound signings and departures;

managerial re-shuffling; constant injuries; the on-going takeover saga and, of course, the frustrating quest for a home league win. In its humour, the book will help to exorcise the memories of a disappointing year in the history of Crystal Palace Football Club.

The future is bright. We have employed a world-class coaching team to steer us back into the Premiership, headed by Terry Venables, and have brought new international quality into the side. Hopefully, once promotion is achieved, the Club will fare better among the big boys. With the team and supporters united, I am sure that we can achieve great things together here at Selhurst Park.

Mark Goldberg

1 - May & June

Hip Hop Hooray!

The Sun, Tuesday, 27 May, 1997

Rob Hawthorne: '...and it's deflected for another corner.'

Alan Brazil: 'Yes, Dean Gordon on his right foot this time, not the left. It just cannons off Tiler and now it's a worrying time for Howard Kendall's Sheffield United. The Palace fans away to our left, out of their seats. Can they win it?'

Hawthorne: 'The corner taken and Simon Rodger floats it in [*voice rises in anticipation*] ...and it's cleared by Tiler again [*deflation*]. David Hopkin, looking to curl one!'

[*Pandemonium breaks out. Palace players converge on Hopkin whose toothless grin and outstretched arms are quickly buried deep beneath his joyful team-mates. One end of Wembley explodes, the other implodes. Hawthorne is barely audible above the wild celebrations*]

'Absolutely amazing! Half a minute to go and Crystal Palace have done to Sheffield United what Leicester did to them a year ago!'

Brazil: 'Would you believe it?' [*Even Brazil is speechless*]

'What a finish from the Scotsman!' [*Veiled attempt to turn Palace's moment of glory into a crusade from the Highlands?*]

'Realising time was ticking...what a finish from the right foot. Tracey, no chance whatsoever. He'll never hit a ball sweeter than that! Top corner. Right out the top drawer.'

'Hopkin surely has won the match for Crystal Palace. Premiership here they come. Fantastic!'

[*The celebrations continue...*]

    And continue they did, long into the night. For Palace fans, that Play-Off Final triumph exorcised the horrors of a year earlier as a shinned effort from Leicester's Steve Claridge looped, painfully slowly, into the top corner of Nigel Martyn's net. Now it no longer mattered. Never again would the chant 'Claridge in the last minute' cause shivers of disappointment to weave their way down the spine. Suddenly, we had 'Hopkin in the last minute', a victory to savour and a promotion plucked from the gaping jaws of the Nationwide League. So it was a dreadful game, a scrappy, tense affair that was begging for that one moment of class. That didn't matter. While even the most ardent Palace fan felt for Sheffield United's followers — everyone knew what they were going through — this victory was about Crystal Palace. The party had just begun.

'At first, it was just sheer disbelief,' recollects Rob Ellis, a Palace fanatic and one of the merrier contingents of the crowd of 64,383 that Bank Holiday Monday. 'Things like that just don't happen to Palace. We don't do last minute winners. We certainly don't do last minute winners at Wembley, anyway. After the elation came a certainty that something must be wrong, that the goal might have been off-side. Something had to be wrong. Then came relief. Relief as the whole season caught us up. It was one of the worst games of the season and the apprehension beforehand had been unbelievable, but when that goal went in it made all those long trips to Grimsby worth it. This is what it is all about!'

That baking hot afternoon under the Twin Towers was significant for many other reasons, perhaps not so apparent at the time and only truly appreciated in hindsight. The team which had taken the Eagles back into the big time had been carefully assembled and expertly crafted by Steve Coppell, Ray Lewington, Peter Nicholas and Dave Bassett over a two year period. It was widely regarded as a promising young side, capable of great things (had not Bassett said as much when rejecting an approach from Manchester City the previous September?) and aided by the wily purchase of 'old head' Andy Linighan and the evergreen Ray Houghton. The mainstays of the side — Hopkin, Dougie Freedman, Andy Roberts, Marc Edworthy, David Tuttle, Bruce Dyer — sported an average age of 23, while Dean Gordon was considered a seasoned campaigner at the tender age of 24. The fact of the matter was that, although Selhurst Park boasted some of the brightest prospects in the Nationwide League, this squad could not hope to keep the Eagles in the top flight. The days when Palace could buy for the future had passed. Experience was needed — perhaps going against Chairman Ron Noades' natural instincts. Undoubtedly, Steve Coppell faced a summer of frantic transfer activity if his squad was to be even marginally capable of surviving its first year back amongst the big spenders of the FA Carling Premiership.

The supporters knew this and, even as the thumping hangovers began to subside, anxious hands throughout SE25 passed over the Alka-Seltzer and picked up the television remotes for *Ceefax* and the long cherished page 302. No longer would Palace be relegated to a mere three-line news brief on page 312. From now on, we could enjoy the fruits of our success, and even perhaps hope for a green headline or, heaven forbid, a coveted spot on pages 303 or 304! Of such madness are dreams made...

The early signs suggested the Eagles' supporters would be rewarded for their faith. Noades had barely relinquished his vice-like grip on the Play-Off trophy, having paraded it around Wembley Stadium in triumph, when he announced that there was money to spend, and Palace would indeed be looking to strengthen the squad significantly over the summer months. The Wembley win had been worth its weight in gold, with television rights alone swelling the coffers to bursting point, to the extent that the press reported Hopkin's strike as being worth in the region of £10 million. While such a sum represents only one 'World class' player in today's inflated market, Palace could conceivably hope to bring in a number of top flight campaigners for such an amount to steer them through the initial, acclimatising skirmishes provided by the Premier League.

So, the scene was set for a summer spending spree, carried on the wave of optimism provided by the Wembley success. If ever a single headline was mercilessly designed to shatter this idyllic illusion, that which awaited Palace fans on television's own 'information super highway' in mid-June was perhaps the cruellest: 'Hopkin in Leeds talks'. While *Ceefax* stuttered its way apologetically towards page 304 — this wasn't the kind of green headline news we had expected after promotion — the realisation that Palace could be about to off-load the inspiration behind their elevation began to sink in. It smacked of Ian Wright's sudden and unexpected departure in 1991. We were all used to star names leaving Selhurst Park, but usually it seemed vaguely justified or understandable — Nigel Martyn left because we had not been promoted; Andy Gray had left after an untimely training ground bust up with the management team; Chris Armstrong and half the Premiership side of 1994/95 had moved on because...well, just because. Hopkin's exit would make no sense. True, he had been continually linked with Leeds ever since an impressive display in an FA Cup third round tie in January 1997 and, true, he had been anxious to break into the Scottish side in time for France '98. But Palace were in the Premiership. Why did he need to move on?

Ron Noades was quick to state publicly that Hopkin had been offered a new contract at Selhurst Park which would financially better anything offered by George Graham. Yet, having travelled to Finland with the rest of the Palace squad for their annual pre-season goal fest, Hopkin returned to sign a £3.25 million deal with the Elland Road outfit. Steve Coppell confirmed the loss: 'We tried our utmost to keep him and I think we offered the same money as Leeds did, but he decided that he wanted to move — and with us looking down the barrel of Bosman (the player having just one year left on his contract) we let him go.

'Perhaps if we'd made our last offer as our first one then he might have signed but, all along as we were pushing to try and keep him, I just felt that he was going to go. He was making all the right noises that Palace had been good to him etc. etc., but there was always a "but". At one stage we just had to say, "He's desperate to go to Leeds so we've got to let go".'

Whether it was good business sense or not, once again Palace had let a key member of their side slip away. Images of Bolton Wanderers letting Jason McAteer leave Burnden Park after promotion in 1995 stood out in the memory - you simply cannot survive in the top flight if you let go of your best players.

Some fans disagreed. Paul Romain, writing in the match day magazine, was quick to point out what an uncharacteristic risk Graham was taking: 'We have made a huge profit on the back of one admittedly good season, but that in the first division and in a free-scoring team'. Such an assessment is entirely fair. Hopkin was undoubtedly a major factor in Palace gaining promotion, not least with that goal at Wembley. However, at Premiership level, he had as much to prove as any of his equally promising team-mates. Alan Brazil, SKY's pundit on that wonderful, sun-drenched day in May, was almost right, although, 'He'll never hit a ball sweeter than that' should have read 'He'll never hit a ball sweeter than that for Palace!'

Romain concluded: 'I suspect that David will struggle to make an impact at Leeds who, as a team, barely managed as many league goals as he did last season! As for giving himself the best chance of playing for Scotland in the World Cup — well, he might have done well to consider the likes of Thomas, McGoldrick, Shaw, Salako and even Martyn, all of whom sought greener grass and international rewards with a conspicuous lack of success. Perhaps far better to be a big fish in a small pond?' Prophetic words indeed when one considers that the midfielder, having initially been made captain of Graham's expensively assembled squad, ended 1998/99 without a first team place and, as a result, was a good deal further down the pecking order in Craig Brown's eyes for the international side. Without senior appearances behind him, Hopkin missed out on much and, at the time of writing, could well be on the way out of Elland Road after just one season in Yorkshire. Sadly, Palace's loss was no one's gain.

So June, which had promised so much, was threatening to turn into something approaching disaster for Steve Coppell and his squad-building exercise. The Mitcham training ground had been flooded with trialists from the farthest flung parts of the globe - footballing outposts, previously unheard of, were suddenly producing players 'desperate' to join the Eagles. Unfortunately, some actually did. More worrying was the steady list of departures from Selhurst: Hopkin to Leeds; Houghton to Reading on a free transfer; Andy Cyrus to Exeter; Chris Day to Watford. The latter's move to Vicarage Road at least saw Kevin Miller travel in the opposite direction in a deal worth around £1.55 million, although one of the chief satisfactions in completing the Cornishman's transfer was to prevent Nottingham Forest getting their man. Former Selhurst boss Dave Bassett had thought Miller was bound for the City Ground, only for Steve Coppell to pull off the deal from under the Midlanders' noses. At this point, Bassett's mid-season departure from South London a few months earlier caused much merriment with the clubs trading places in the élite. Each would enjoy contrasting seasons.

Nevertheless, the feeling of anti-climax was becoming tangible as the summer wore on. Had we not learned from the experiences of 1994? Where were the promised big-name signings? Above all, was Steve Coppell genuinely 'happy with the squad' he had largely inherited, as reported in the national press? That comment was almost the straw that broke the ('recently promoted into a league and potentially totally out of its depth') camel's back. It was patently obvious that a side which had barely scraped into the end of season play-offs - already minus its two most influential midfielders and long established as the bookies' favourites for the drop - would hardly raise a murmur in the Premier League.

It seemed the malaise had also reached the players. Even in Finland, the customary cricket score thrashings never materialised, while the indifferent form continued into the domestic programme of friendlies. The omens did not look good, and coach Ray Lewington gloomily predicted Palace's immediate demise if new players were not brought in before the season started. In response, Palace's *Clubcall* service went into overload (perhaps trying to shake the management and chairman out of their slumber) and began linking the Eagles with a host of foreign stars, each as wildly unrealistic and fantastic as the next.

'Baggio to join Eagles?' — highly unlikely. 'Gascoigne on his way' — blink and you missed that one. 'Eagles swoop for Lombardo?' — the icing on the cake. How ridiculous was that? Smiling ruefully at such preposterous speculation, Palace fans reverted to reading about Marc Overmars (£7 million), Stan Collymore (£7 million), Alessandro Pistone (£4.3 million), Paul Ince (£4.2 million) and Les Ferdinand (£6 million). Now here was money really being thrown about, although by no means all of it wisely. Regardless, it was international talent commanding fees the Eagles could only dream of. What chances Palace signing someone of the stature of Lombardo? He probably didn't even know where Crystal Palace was.

Still, we could only dream...

2 - July & August

JUST ONE LOMBARDO

Crystal Palace travelling fans, Goodison Park,
9 August, 1997

Attilio Lombardo is instantly recognisable to football fans all over the globe. It is to the Italian's eternal misfortune, however, that such fame is as much the result of his bald pate as his undoubted footballing skills. Attilio is markedly unrepresentative of Italian football — no chiselled features, no noticeable tan and, above all, no slicked back, elaborately coiffeured hair. He is follicularly challenged to a degree that George Dawes would envy while, next to Lombardo, Bobby Charlton boasts a positive thatch.

Yet, Lombardo is a star. While at Sampdoria, James Richardson and his *Channel 4* team seemed magnetically drawn to the flying winger. Admittedly, 'Samp' was the team of the moment during much of Attilio's time in Genoa, but it was the relationship between Lombardo and Gianluca Vialli which made them tick. In a strange way, Lombardo and Vialli have fascinated Italian audiences for the same reason — their respective, and distinctive, hair-styles: Gianluca with his constantly changing bouffant; Attilio with his total lack of one. Regardless, whenever you flicked into *Football Italia* on a Sunday afternoon, there was Lombardo tearing down the right wing in the distinctive blue strip. The man-of-the-match awards piled up, but he seemed unlikely ever to play for his country — his appearance seemed so much against him.

Of course, I do the Italian FA an injustice. Lombardo did break into the international set-up and enjoyed a spell in the *Azzurri*, which made the sudden link with newly-promoted Crystal Palace all the more bizarre. Ironically, the Lombardo rumours surfaced immediately after Palace's *Clubcall* service had linked the Eagles with Roberto Baggio. Did Lombardo represent a step down in the Club's ambitions? More to the point, did the Club genuinely entertain hopes of luring the cream of *Football Italia* to SE25? What was going on?

Suggestions of a shock swoop appeared scotched by manager Steve Coppell's insight into Palace's pre-Premiership transfer policy: 'I don't want to end up with some mercenary foreign player who's just come over here for the money. The players we sign will be British players.'

Coach Ray Lewington was equally cautious about the possibility of the Italian joining. 'His arrival would be an exciting prospect,' he said, trying not to sound too hopeful. 'It worries me sometimes that we look for "names" now. I know there have been a few who have been successful, but there are quite a few who haven't.' Perhaps common sense was prevailing, much to most people's disappointment. So, while Chelsea and Arsenal added to their foreign imports, Palace scoured the domestic transfer scene and tentatively opened talks with Blackburn Rovers for the purchase of Paul Warhurst.

Chairman Ron similarly appeared to quash the Lombardo speculation. 'I have never favoured the foreign players,' he told *Clubcall*. 'At Palace we like our players home-grown, home-bought and with a sell-on figure.' Noades subsequently reaffirmed this strategy by plucking the previously unknown Jamie Fullarton, ironically from FC Bastia of Corsica, on a free transfer. Fullarton was 22 years of age, had attracted interest from Glasgow Celtic and was undoubtedly 'one for the future', *ie:* excellent business. Yet, surely this was a major signing for the Nationwide League Crystal Palace, and not the Premiership hopefuls of 1997/98. Derby and Leicester, who had both comfortably survived their first year in the Premiership, had each broken their transfer records in order to guarantee such survival. Admittedly, the Foxes had concentrated on home-based players and a Wimbledonesque fighting spirit, but the £1.6 million spent on Matt Elliott of Oxford was a major investment which had paid off handsomely.

All this seemed to suggest that Lombardo would not be gracing the Premiership when the season kicked off in under a month's time — unless of course Palace's apparent interest was mirrored by more established 'glamour' clubs looking to strengthen their right-hand flank. However, it seemed that the chief motivation behind the scenes to secure the Italian's signature did not come from Noades, nor even from Coppell (although both undoubtedly would have liked to welcome an international star of Attilio's calibre to the Club), but from a new face on the scene — Mark Goldberg. A millionaire and chairman of a computer firm based in Bromley, Goldberg was a life-long Palace fan who, like Noades, seemed intent on developing Selhurst Park into a super stadium and leisure complex as well as providing funds for new players. It seemed no coincidence that, on the day he joined the Palace board of directors, the Lombardo rumours first hit the news stands.

Suffice to say, Goldberg was something of an unknown quantity to supporters and media men alike. Indeed, the most anyone appeared to know of him was where his company was based. The new director must have become increasingly bored with the constant references to 'the Bromley-based businessman...' over the coming months in every article, programme note or news brief about his plans for the Club. Perhaps here was the sugar-daddy Palace had always lacked to break into the élite? Of course, Goldberg's influence would become more evident as the season progressed. Significantly though, and even at this early stage, if he wanted Attilio to join Palace, maybe all was not lost.

Palace had brought in Premiership quality in Warhurst by the time the Lombardo rumours resurfaced in mid-July. This time there seemed more substance to the story, with the Club reportedly having agreed a fee of £2.1 million, leaving the small matter of the Italian's personal terms as the only possible stumbling block. But what a stumbling block they could be!

Twelve months earlier, Attilio Lombardo had been on the brink of joining David Pleat's Sheffield Wednesday for a similar fee. However, his insistence on a salary of £1.7 million had prompted the Hillsborough outfit to pull out of the deal at the last moment. Graham Mackrell, the Yorkshire club's secretary, stated: 'The player's expectations were such that we had to pull out. We are not prepared to pay crazy money.' In July 1997, Palace's transfer record stood at £2.2 million, paid to Millwall for newly-appointed skipper Andy Roberts and, logically, they would almost double that outlay if they were to sign Lombardo for one season. Regardless of which division Palace were playing in, this was a different league.

On 24 July, the media reported that the deal had fallen through due to the player's excessive wage requirements, as well as on almost surreal demands allegedly made by Lombardo from his home in Turin. Steve Coppell explained: 'We established what the player was looking for, but there was a misunderstanding about gross and net and, when we realised that, we quickly came to the conclusion that we could not compete'.

Fair enough. The transfer had been scuppered on a mistranslation. It's easily done. Coppell continued: 'My gut feeling at the moment is that the deal looks likely to break down because of the size of the whole package. It would be a lot of money for us.' All this, Palace fans could understand. We did not buy international stars every day of the week because we simply could not afford to — that was obvious — and partly explains why the news of Lombardo's possible transfer had caused such a stir. It was the news that the Italian had apparently demanded a maid and luxury country mansion (only if a castle in the heart of Surrey proved unobtainable, mind you) that struck us all as odd. Had he any idea what South London was like? A luxury mansion on the outskirts of Turin is one thing, but in South Norwood?

'I was not asking for the moon,' Lombardo responded to Coppell's pessimistic line. Thank God. At least the maid wouldn't need a separate oxygen supply. 'It is no secret that I am earning £600,000 a year at Juventus and no Italian player has ever gone to England before without getting more money than he was earning in Italy. Why should I be different? If we had all sat around a table together, I bet we could have come to an agreement immediately. I still hope the situation can be resolved within days.'

Did he know anything about the Club he was supposedly so keen on joining? Apparently not. He knew that Palace had recently been promoted to the Premiership, but he had not heard of them prior to the Wembley win and had no idea whereabouts in London they played. Memories of Bulgarian goalkeeper Bobby Mihailov's gross misunderstanding prior to joining Reading sprang to mind. The international 'keeper had allegedly watched the Royals' Play-Off Final defeat at the hands of Bolton in 1996 and presumed

Wembley Stadium was Reading's home ground. Even Uri Geller would be hard pressed to convince anyone of that. Back in reality, on the day when Paul Warhurst finally completed all the formalities of a move from Blackburn Rovers — which itself involved a huge upheaval for a player whose heart has always been in the north — the long-running Lombardo saga appeared to be drawing to an unhappy close. The deal was as good as dead.

On Tuesday, 29 July, Palace travelled to Craven Cottage to play their penultimate pre-season friendly. Micky Adams' talented young Cottagers had recently celebrated their promotion to the Second Division and were looking forward to a year of consolidation — at least before Messrs Al Fayed, Keegan and (the Eagles' recently re-appointed coach) Ray Wilkins arrived on the scene in late September. Palace fielded Miller in goal, although their only other major incoming transfer, Paul Warhurst, was still absent from South London. Perhaps the performance on the banks of the Thames was a reaction to the thrashing handed out to local rivals Millwall just three days earlier, but Coppell's charges were more than a little lucky to emerge victorious by the narrowest of margins after an uninspiring spectacle.

Neil Shipperley scored the only goal. Andy Roberts and Marc Edworthy were as hard-working as ever. Bruce Dyer ran his heart out. Yet, for all that, a member of the crowd was the subject of the most vociferous chanting. Early in the game — with neither side threatening and just as spectators were beginning to question the sense in forking out good money to watch what was, in essence, a protracted fitness exercise — a travelling fan sheepishly arrived in the away end, almost apologetic at the fact that he had missed the start of the game and thus not shared in his fellow fans' boredom. Bedecked in Palace colours and bald as the day he was born, he now took his place towards the front of the terrace. Suddenly, the Palace followers became conscious of the late-arrival's pate and, to a person, issued a rousing chorus of 'Lombar-do, Lombar-do, Lombar-do!' The supporter, pleased at his new found celebrity status, turned and milked the adulation. At least it took our minds off the snail's pace proceedings on the pitch. Indeed, some of the Palace players might have been forgiven for turning round in search of their Italian saviour, come to deliver them from their pre-season torpor. Unfortunately, all realised that this could be the closest we ever came to seeing Lombardo in a Palace shirt. What had we been thinking?

Then again, never underestimate the draw of the Premiership these days. SKY's money has allowed English top-flight football to become the stage on which to perform, and Lombardo was not going to pass up a chance like this just because he didn't have a clue who he was signing for, or even where they played. I exaggerate. Attilio and Gianluca Vialli are close friends and it seems likely that, in the interim period, the pair discussed whether a big-money switch to South London would be a sensible career move. Perhaps the lure of the capital was significant. How many times have big-name foreign players expressed a desire for a move to a 'London' club as opposed to an 'English' club in recent times? Apart from being a rich man's glamorous playground, London was home to Vialli, Zola, Di Matteo; to Guillit, Wenger, Bergkamp; to Overmars, Lebœuf, Ginola, Petrescu; in other words, to the cream of European footballing talent. Admittedly, it still fell far short of Milan and Turin, but it was catching up. Fast.

Flying in to Biggin Hill airport on a typical British summer's day must have opened Lombardo's eyes up to the prospect of a move to 'swinging London town'. Having allegedly revised his contractual demands, the Italian met with Ron Noades and Steve Coppell (and presumably director Mark Goldberg as well) at a secret location in Croydon and thrashed out a £1.6 million deal. Two days later, on 2 August 1998, and to a collective thud of dropped bacon sandwiches, Attilio was a Crystal Palace player and Coppell was eulogising about his new man: 'He's really enthusiastic and looking forward to the challenge of playing in the Premier League. He's a top international player who is very flexible and will give us that little bit of class, that little bit of guile we may have been missing. It was the total package that was the stumbling block initially, but Juventus reduced their demands and Attilio has also bent our way and made it obvious that he does want to play for us.'

Exactly who had funded the purchase of the player — enabling the Eagles to pull off one of their greatest ever transfer coups — remained something of a mystery until Ron Noades spoke out later in the year. 'All the transfer fees for players brought in were paid by the club,' he insisted. 'We had people talking about Mark Goldberg coming in and being the next chairman of Palace, some saying he'd put other money into the Club which he hadn't and that he'd signed Lombardo — which he hadn't. He certainly helped, because he's got a marketing rights company of his own which has given a contract to Lombardo. And I believe he's probably got contracts with other players here — that's nothing to do with me. But if it helps in any way...'

Goldberg suggested much the same on Palace's *Clubcall* service: 'Knowing that Lombardo was available, and the fact that I come from a recruitment background, I was able to utilise the experience I had in bringing the player to London and negotiating his terms. I was also able to sponsor the player to help make it happen. This came about before I was a director of Crystal Palace and Ron Noades was more than happy for me to get involved at that stage.' There we go then. Clear as mud.

So the Bald Eagle had finally landed. No English, no airs and graces — Attilio let his feet do the talking, and so sweetly did they do so on his first few outings that even opposition fans warmed to his performances. After the media's allegations of exorbitant demands and a somewhat mercenary attitude, the 31-year-old was anxious to make a good impression in his new surroundings.

'The original discussions were just club to club,' he stated, looking back on the press reports. 'When we did talk, I never made any demands for a mansion or a butler. That's not in keeping with my personality at all. I'd like to know who invented such stories because they must have created the wrong impression of me. People must have thought a prima donna was coming to Crystal Palace, when that's never been me at all.'

Maid or no maid, Lombardo trained with his new team-mates for a week before making the trip to Goodison Park for the season's opener on Merseyside. On the two previous occasions back in the top division, Palace had been comfortably defeated at Loftus Road (2-0) in 1989 and unceremoniously stuffed at home to Liverpool (6-1) in 1994. However, insofaras that no match is an 'easy match' in the Premier League, the infamous fixture computer had handed the Eagles a relatively kind outing for the first Saturday. Everton had recently begun their latest spell under the management of Howard Kendall — still smarting no doubt from Hopkin's goal at Wembley — and had only slightly swelled their ranks, with Slaven Bilic and John Oster becoming Toffees over the summer. For Palace, the trio of Miller, Warhurst and Lombardo started their first games for the Club, while Jamie Fullarton found himself on the bench. Over the ensuing ninety minutes, Everton were taught a footballing lesson by the flying Italian, and a new song by the travelling army from South London.

'Just one Lombardo, give him to me...'

The Italian runs on to a Warhurst through-ball and calmly slots past Neville Southall in the Everton goal with the outside of his right foot. Everton 0 Palace 1.

'He's from Juventus in Italy...'

Lombardo tears down the left side of the Everton penalty area and is tripped by the beleaguered Bilic. The referee points to the spot and Bruce Dyer places the ball beyond Southall. Everton 0 Palace 2.

'He's got no hair, but we don't care...'

Despite a late Ferguson consolation, Lombardo's brilliance and a resilient team performance see the Eagles off to their best start in the top flight since 1971. The travelling fans salute a new hero.

'We've got Lombardo, from Italy!'

With Bolton also putting in a solid away-day performance, winning 1-0 at the Dell, the Premiership new boys could look forward with a degree of confidence to the coming season. The Palace manager, meanwhile, was on cloud nine at Lombardo's startling initial impression. 'He just wants to be one of the boys,' he told reporters after the Everton win. 'He is not just here to take the cream. He provided us all with a lift when he arrived and I think he will have a positive effect on others at the Club because, the way he plays, he makes demands of those around him'.

While those demands became evident at home to Barnsley three days later — when Lombardo was so obviously on another footballing plane to those around him that it was almost embarrassing — he continued to flourish away from Selhurst Park. Palace played no better all season than in the first half at Elland Road, and Lombardo rounded off a magnificent team display with a magical second goal as David Hopkin held his head in the centre circle. Watching Leeds, with their numerous Palace connections, struggling to contain a rampant visiting side, seemed to be something of a watershed. Suddenly, life didn't seem so cruel after all.

3 - September

MAULED BY THE TIGERS!

Hull City travelling fans at Selhurst Park, Tuesday, 30 September, 1997

In many ways, August had been a honeymoon for Crystal Palace Football Club. We, the players and supporters, had graduated to a new League in which we were expected to struggle, but had acquitted ourselves fairly well. Furthermore, we had ploughed money heavily into the transfer market — more heavily than at any other time in the Club's history — and brought so many new faces to South London that match days were spent gauging just who could be turning out for the Eagles this week. So that's why the Premier League introduced a squad numbering system! It wasn't a money-spinning exercise, but a means of allowing fans (and management) to work out just who was out there at 3.00pm on a Saturday afternoon. It all makes perfect sense now...

Attilio Lombardo naturally wore the number seven shirt. He was still finding his feet in a new country and culture, but at first his presence seemed to cause more confusion among his team-mates as they tried, and usually failed, to read his mind and anticipate the next defence-splitting pass. Number eight was Paul Warhurst, who had also looked a class act, but was now betraying the early signs of another season of injury problems. His goal at Leeds had proved his quality and, in early September, he seemed Palace's most natural target-man to lead the line.

Of the other new arrivals, Kevin Miller claimed the goalkeeper's jersey and thus relegated crowd favourite and Wembley hero Carlo Nash to the bench. Many felt for Carlo, but presumed he would taste the Premiership at some point over the course of the season. Youngsters Jamie Fullarton (no 26) and Hermann Hreidarsson (no 22) — the latter signed from the marvellously named IBV Knattspyrnurad in Iceland — were 'ones for the future'. Worrying, then, that both would establish themselves in the team before the end of the month. While the shirt list rose to around 40 and the more experienced members of the youth team, this was perhaps more of a psychological ploy to convince Steve Coppell that the squad was large enough to sustain a Premiership place. The £1.2 million Israeli midfielder, Itzik Zohar, appeared to be the last of those challenging for a senior place at number 27.

Still, the big money arrivals did not end here. Neil Emblen, who had been part of the Wolverhampton set-up swept aside by Coppell's boys *en route* to the Premiership, was signed for a fee of £2 million towards the end of August. This sum was more than that paid to Juventus for Lombardo, for a player who had never graced the top flight, reflecting the inflationary nature of the domestic transfer scene. Ironically, the move hardly raised a murmur in the national press. On *Ceefax* the Emblen deal did not merit more than a five-line paragraph on page 312. Did the hacks not realise that Palace still don't sign £2 million players every day of the week? Everyone else might, but we were Crystal Palace and didn't. Or maybe we did nowadays...

'I just felt that you can't be exposed at the back in Premiership football with players who are untried and untested,' confirmed the manager. 'Okay, we've got Andy Linighan, Tutts and Hermann — whom we've got high hopes for, but we don't know how he's going to develop yet — but Neil can play at the back and can also release somebody from midfield to play at the back if need be. He gives us more options.' A squad player? Costing £2 million?!

Perhaps the whole scenario should be put into context. Emblen's signing was just the latest stage of Palace ascending into the big time. On previous outings into the Premier League, precious little money had been spent on improving the squad, mainly because the strength of those already at the Club was deemed sufficient to guarantee survival. Only Andy Preece, Darren Pitcher and Rhys Whilmot had joined in the summer of 1994 (and Ray Wilkins, who signs for Palace whenever they are promoted to the Premiership and tends to move on again after a month or two) for a combined fee well short of £1 million — a sum paid out for a Premiership reserve team player nowadays who has never made a senior appearance.

Third time around, however, the painful lessons had been learned. Indeed, necessity dictated that new players had to be brought in. On the previous two campaigns in the Premiership, Palace had been expected to flourish — either as an already established top-flight outfit, or as convincing champions of the entire Football League. This time, however, a side that had struggled even to gain entry into the First Division play-offs was not going to be in for an easy ride against the bottomless-pocketed clubs of SKY's glamour division. Palace were favourites to finish 20th in 1997/98, while Steve Coppell was 5-4 on to be the first manager to lose his job. Enough said.

Then again, it wasn't just about bringing expensive new players to the Club. Off the pitch, Palace were developing a distinctly 'Premier League' experience for the fans to enjoy. *Palace Radio* broadcast live match commentaries and phone-ins from Norwood to Coulsdon. So it wasn't Jonathan Pearce's transportations of delight over a glorious Palace triumph on *Capital Gold*; it wasn't even Alan Green bemoaning another miserable night at Selhurst Park on *Radio Five Live*; but it was all about the Eagles and, above all, it was pretty good. Meanwhile, *Clubcall* went from strength to strength and was nationally credited as the seventh most telephoned site on the football information network, behind a handful of big-spending glamour clubs like Manchester United, Leeds and Chelsea.

Even the news stalls suddenly found a niche for the boys in red and blue as *Eagles* magazine entered the market against already existing glossy covers from Chelsea and Manchester United. Were we tapping the 'fair weather fans' market? At last it was possible to visit Sainsbury's at Selhurst Park and buy a magazine about Crystal Palace Football Club, as opposed to that of a side based at the other end of the country. Whether *Eagles* magazine would have sold quite so well in Newcastle remains something of a moot point.

On the marketing side — an area alien to most die-hard supporters, but a necessary spin-off from football's popularity nowadays — Palace continued to progress. Regardless of how one feels about corporate hospitality's sudden and dramatic influence on the game, Phil Alexander and his marketing team excelled in attracting new businesses to the Club and therefore generated many of the funds subsequently ploughed back into the team. Sporting dinners, corporate events and match day hospitality reached levels never previously seen at Selhurst Park which has, after all, boasted a top-flight Club of some description since the mid-1980s.

All this progress reflected the development of the national game since Palace had last been a Premier League club in 1994/95. The Club was jumping on the band-wagon and, for once, the supporters were actually benefiting. What was important was that Palace remained at this elevated level, and that's where the problems began. It's all very well having a Premiership set-up off the pitch, but it's down to the team to guarantee that the Club competes in the appropriate division — Manchester City, Sunderland, Middlesbrough and Nottingham Forest, to name just four clubs boasting huge resources, all found themselves 'Premiership clubs' with First Division teams playing in the Nationwide League in 1997. For City, the misery didn't end there.

The boardroom, much as it would like to, could not guarantee top flight football after Palace's first season back under Andy Gray's high-tech video surveillance. Two of September's fixtures served to indicate just how long the road was going to be to establish Palace as a Premier club.

On Saturday, 13 September 1997, Chelsea visited Selhurst Park with their array of foreign stars. The last time the Blues played Palace in the Premiership on the Eagles' home soil, their most frightening prospect up front was Paul Furlong — a prospect which proved too much for Alan Smith's side, as the muscular target man enjoyed a rare moment of glory in Chelsea colours by netting the only goal of the game. Things had changed somewhat since then. The Stamford Bridge revolution, initiated by Glenn Hoddle, was well under way with Ruud Guillit at the helm and the visitors on this occasion boasted a Dutchman in goal; a Romanian, a Frenchman and two Englishmen across the back; three (yes, three!) Englishmen and a Uruguayan across the middle; and a Welshman and Norwegian up front. On the bench, the Blues rested a trio of Italian internationals in Gianluca Vialli, Gianfranco Zola and Roberto Di Matteo. Not a bad bunch of musketeers to bring on just in case the side yet to win at home gets a bit too cocky!

Palace, meanwhile, had been robbed of the services of Warhurst and Edworthy, giving Neil Emblen his first start. Attilio shared a joke with his fellow countrymen before kick-off, perhaps along the lines of, 'You should have joined Palace — at least you'd get into the side'. In reality, Chelsea's Cup Winners' Cup commitments probably ensured the threesome's absence, and could well have spared the home side further embarrassment. Regardless, the crowd was swollen to a season's best 26,186 on a bright, hot, sunny day. Chelsea were in town — a London derby against one of the most attractive footballing sides in the country. This was what the Premier League was all about.

By 4.45 pm that afternoon, most Palace fans wished they had never had to find out exactly what the Premier League was about at all. Chelsea had strolled — no more than that — to a comfortable 3-0 win thanks to a typical Mark Hughes volley, a Frank Lebœuf penalty (both before the half-hour mark) and a Graeme Le Saux cracker in the last minute. Thank you and goodnight. Bruce Dyer's near-post header was about as close as the home side had come but, in reality, the defeat had seemed on the cards as soon as the Italians had been named on the visiting bench. It was almost as if Guillit had decided 'We don't need Vialli, Zola and Di Matteo to beat this lot. Mark Nicholls, Paul Hughes and Tore Andre Flo should do it comfortably'. I suppose he was right.

'It's weird. When we used to lose in the Nationwide League, I would get wound up because it was obvious that we weren't playing as well as we could,' reflects Rob Ellis, looking back on that balmy September afternoon... well, for Chelsea fans anyway. 'The Chelsea game was just one of those days when everybody sat there in the pub afterwards and went, "Well, we were just not good enough". We were outclassed. You couldn't criticise the players, it was just that Chelsea were on a different level. We all sat there and thought what the hell are we doing in a division with teams like that?'

Similar sentiments were expressed by Paul Romain in his match day programme article at the Bolton Wanderers fixture. 'I've made the point before that we have to expect to lose to teams like Chelsea and Blackburn. The trick is in not allowing those defeats to lead to a run of poor results against teams we must beat to survive.'

Since the start of the campaign, Palace had lost to Barnsley and Southampton by one-nil margins. Coppell's men had been unlucky at the Dell, where a perfectly legitimate penalty appeal had been mysteriously turned down and, in a way, equally unfortunate against the Tykes. After all, no one could have forseen Neil Redfearn's glorious goal midway through the second period. Perhaps the word had not reached the players that, as a former Eagle, Redfearn would inevitably score that night, but that he would do it with such style, no one could have forecast. The other defeat came at the hands of a rampant Blackburn Rovers side who were currently flying high at the Premiership summit under the watchful eye of another former Palace player — local man, Roy Hodgson. The second-half performance against Rovers had promised much and therefore softened the disappointment of the defeat. No, it wasn't until the Chelsea fixture that the gulf between the Football League and the Premiership really became apparent.

Steve Coppell confirmed as much at the time: 'I think we have to realise that there are certain teams in this division against which, if we say, "You have the ball and have a go, then we'll have the ball and have a go," then we're going to get beaten. Heavily. On the day I just think they were too good for us. We struggle more against the teams who pass it around and keep possession and invariably those are the better sides. I was quoted as saying "Oh shit!" when I saw the quality of the players on the Chelsea bench, but in reality I was well pleased that the Italians weren't starting!' Heaven knows how many the visitors would have scored if all their international stars had featured. As it was, Palace would discover the true extent of the Blues' resources when they visited Stamford Bridge the following March. Then there would be no hiding from the *Azzurri*'s menace.

In keeping with Romain's comment that one bad defeat must not lead to a series of poor results, the side picked themselves up well following the Chelsea drubbing. A Lombardo goal saw off Wimbledon in an 'away' fixture at Selhurst, while Jamie Fullarton's speculative effort tied things up at Highfield Road. Admittedly, only a point at home to Bolton was disappointing, especially having been 2-0 up, but Coppell stressed how far the side had come along in a short period. On paper, the visit of Bolton had, six months earlier, been Palace's toughest test of the season. Suddenly it had become one of the easiest as expectations altered dramatically. Still, eleven points by the end of October was no disgrace and saw the Eagles comfortably in mid-table. However, taking the League programme in isolation would ignore one of the most alarming stages of the campaign — a second round Coca-Cola Cup-tie with Hull City.

Mark Hateley's early days as manager at Boothferry Park had been nondescript to say the least. Apart from a freak 7-4 triumph over Swansea City, with a quintet of goals from Duane Darby, there had been literally nothing to cheer about. The club was 91st in the Football League and only likely to avoid the ultimate disappointment if Doncaster's desperate plummet into oblivion continued in earnest (which, of course, it did). Against clubs like this, Premier sides triumph convincingly. If ever Palace needed to be reminded of their true status in the grand scheme of things, then a 1-0 defeat on Humberside should have amply served its purpose.

The Eagles won few friends with that loss to Darby's 28th minute goal. While conceding that lower league clubs regularly cause upsets in the various cup competitions, it was the nature of the defeat that really riled. Paul Romain took up the argument in the programme for the return leg: 'When Hull scored, the Palace substitutes were warming up in front of our seats. Far from offering any sort of moral support at this turn of events by a shout of encouragement to anybody on the pitch, a couple of them appeared to find the whole thing rather funny. Meanwhile, none of the excessive number of people on the Palace bench seemed to be in the slightest bit agitated at any stage of a match we clearly weren't performing well in.'

So the Palace players and management did not appear to be 'up for' the match. This, of course, is open to (no doubt heated) debate, but what was very clear was that the side taking to the field was noticeably below strength. Whether players were injured or not remains a mystery, but the lack of depth in the squad, despite multi-million pound arrivals over the previous few months, was alarming. Romain was sceptical: 'I have to say I find it a coincidence that we are complaining of not having the luxury of resting Lombardo on Saturday against Chelsea, and then a mysterious injury keeps him out at Hull - an injury which was apparent to nobody on Saturday last and which, unsurprisingly, had disappeared by Saturday next.'

However, yet more disturbing was the second leg of the tie at Selhurst Park on 30 September. With the prospect of a trip to Newcastle United awaiting the winners, surely both clubs would be eager to progress to the next stage of the competition. I dare say both sides were but, over two matches, you would have thought true skill would ultimately have triumphed, wouldn't you? In the event, another weakened Palace line-up took to the pitch and proceeded to concede an elementary goal from a set piece (to someone called Ian Wright of all people!) to be trailing 1-0 at half-time. Carl Veart — a workman-like midfielder who would never profess to be in the Lombardo or Hopkin mould, despite the unrealistic expectations of some fans in August — capped an otherwise ordinary performance with the equaliser and George Ndah's half-volley set up extra-time.

Surely Palace's Premier ambitions would prevail in the added half-hour. Well, they didn't and the Eagles had been well and truly 'mauled by the Tigers,' as we were continually reminded by the large band of travelling supporters. The débâcle had been witnessed by 6,407 people — almost 3,000 fewer than had watched the loss at Boothferry Park. A subsequent reversal of UEFA's policy, allowing the Coca-Cola Cup winners to enter European competition, rubbed salt into the wounds gouged by Hateley's claws. The two-legged defeat, on away goals, left an air of unreality at Selhurst. Twelve months earlier and at the same stage, promotion-chasing Bury had been swept aside 7-1 on aggregate by a virtually identical side riding on the crest of a wave. How a year changes things in football.

Significantly, however, the games at home to Chelsea and Hull City really put Palace's ambitions into perspective. To become a 'Premier club', we needed more than just a 'premier' set-up behind the scenes, big-money signings and our own radio station. We needed to create our own 'premier ideology', to convince ourselves that we were good enough to compete with the best. For a while over the ensuing two months, that is exactly what we did.

4 - October & November

PADOVANO... INVESTED WISELY

The Guardian, Tuesday, 25 November, 1997

Thursday, 13 November. Crystal Palace's first team go down to a narrow 2-1 defeat in a prestige friendly in Sweden against IFK Gothenburg. Neil Shipperley's incredible scoring sequence is extended against the Champions' League representatives and the senior side gain a useful run-out and opportunity to gauge just how much progress they have made since gaining promotion to the English Premiership. Meanwhile, back in South London, Italian international and Juventus star Michele Padovano completes a £1.71 million switch from *Serie A* to the Eagles, renewing acquaintance with his former Juve team-mate, Attilio Lombardo.

Friday, 14 November. Chairman Ron Noades announces to the media that he is willing to sell his stake in the Club to Mark Goldberg for £30 million. A deadline of February 1998 has been set for the IT contract recruitment tycoon to come up with the money, although it appears that 10% of Noades' shares have already been purchased, thus providing the funds to complete the Padovano deal.

Saturday, 15 November. Attilio Lombardo goes down with a hamstring injury while training for the World Cup qualifying play-off with Russia in Rome. He seems set for a lengthy spell on the sidelines. Possible replacements are mentioned — the usual suspects: Brolin, Gascoigne, Signori, Dave, Pete...

Just your average week at Crystal Palace Football Club, then. While October and November were relatively quiet months on the playing side, the Club seemed to compensate by finding new and improved ways of forcing its way into the media spotlight. Whether it be multi-million pound arrivals, mass departures to the Nationwide League, possible financial takeovers involving Italian giants and intricate, if not mysterious, business dealings or the continued pursuit of Croydon Council's approval to develop the Main Stand, Palace were never far from the news. As if holding your own in tenth place in the Premiership wasn't enough to keep everyone happy!

In retrospect, perhaps more should have been made of the team's impressive form at the time. The heady days of a top-half placing seem a distant memory now, but Palace undoubtedly merited their elevated position. A 2-0 reverse at Old Trafford had drawn criticism — most of it grossly unfair — but had been followed with a gritty, goalless draw with table-topping Arsenal, a convincing win at Hillsborough, a floodlight failure at Upton Park and fine performances against Aston Villa and 'Spurs. The four points gained in those two fixtures, while they could and should have been six, propelled Steve Coppell's side well clear of danger. The defence seemed water-tight by comparison to those of Wednesday, 'Spurs, Bolton and Barnsley, while Richard Keys and Andy Gray were positively salivating over the deserved victory at White Hart Lane in front of SKY's cameras. Indeed, Jonathan Pearce went so far as to cite Marc Edworthy's charge down the flank in the 57th minute, which set up the goal, as the best forward run by a full-back he had ever seen. No fluke was responsible for the Eagles' success.

All this is not bad for a side accused of being 'gutless, scared, lacklustre and unambitious' at Old Trafford on 4 October, just three days after the Premiership champions had been unlucky to have triumphed only 3-2 against Juventus in the same arena. Those comments came from one disgruntled fan in the local press, although it is unlikely the same fan was complaining about Coppell's tactics a few weeks later, as the Eagles romped to victory in South Yorkshire.

'After the Manchester United game I felt a little bit disappointed about the criticism that we'd approached the game defensively,' revealed the Palace manager. 'We got a fair amount of praise after Sheffield Wednesday and yet we played exactly the same shape and the same way against both teams. It's just that against United, you get pressed back. I find these conflicting views very interesting reading for us sometimes.'

Those endorsing a more cavalier approach at Old Trafford need look no further than the heavy defeats the Red Devils inflicted upon Barnsley and Wednesday in October (7-0 and 6-1). Conversely, the only 'surprise' defeat suffered by Alex Ferguson's men on home territory throughout the 1997/98 season came at the hands of Leicester City, and it's unlikely Martin O'Neill's last words before his team took to the field that afternoon were 'Attack, attack, attack!'

The manager's tactics made perfect sense. Defence had emerged as the side's true forte, with Miller excelling behind a solid marking unit, which extended into midfield *via* the tigerish tackling of Simon Rodger and captain Andy Roberts. Hermann Hreidarsson, so ungainly in pre-season, had dispelled rumours suggesting he was another Leif Andersen (incredibly worth over £4 million on Domark's PC game, *Championship Manager 2*. What were they thinking?) to establish himself as the bargain buy of the year. He recovered from an unfortunate own goal in Manchester well enough to disrupt Dennis Bergkamp's rhythm at Selhurst Park, provoking a rash tackle and a three-match suspension for the sole entrant in *Match of the Day*'s popular competition 'Bergkamp of the Month'. While Des and Gary pondered just who might provide them with ten curled efforts into the top left hand corner while the Dutchman was on the sidelines, Palace continued to harry and work feverishly to earn a deserved point.

How we chuckled to ourselves, especially as Arsène Wenger bemoaned the lack of protection for his Dutch star. 'Their number 22 [super

Hermann the Viking] did so many fouls on Bergkamp but was never punished. There were times when he had both of his hands around Dennis for as long as six or seven seconds. I can understand why Dennis gets upset and frustrated.'

Coppell's riposte was speedy and perfectly delivered: 'I can't understand how Wenger can claim we were physical when his team had five bookings and we had one.' At the time, it was refreshing to welcome Arsène to the British game, even when the alleged 'treatment' had been handed out by another import. A few months later, Wenger had probably proved he had adapted rather better to the more physical side to the game over here... or even risen well above it in claiming the Gunners' 'double'.

Against the other North London giants, Tottenham Hotspur, Palace fared even better, as Shipperley's goal saw Christian Gross immediately turn, in desperation, for the hair dye. Watching the new 'Spurs boss's reaction to the 1-0 reverse must have been painful for the most die-hard Tottenham fan. Never before has a manager seemed so out of his depth — so longing for the homely comforts of his native land — after only one competitive match. Maybe he should have considered asking Alan Sugar to change the club name to Grasshopper Hotspur, just to make North London feel slightly more like his beloved Zurich. Regardless, it was hard not to feel smug, having extinguished all optimism from the Lane after such an impressive away-day showing.

So, despite the lack of a home win, the side was performing well on the pitch and betrayed no signs of the wheels falling off — as had apparently already occurred at Oakwell, White Hart Lane and Hillsborough. In the wider scheme of things, however, it was events off the pitch which made October and November more significant in the context of Palace's season and its future. These months saw the continuing break-up of the promotion-winning side — a process that had started in the summer with the release of Houghton, Day and Hopkin, and continued with a vengeance until Andy Roberts' switch to Wimbledon in February. Admittedly, these were short-term decisions which upset many of the supporters, but they reflected a more integral and wide-reaching change at the Club. The takeover saga had begun in earnest.

The 'power struggle', if that indeed is what it was, between Ron Noades and Mark Goldberg centred on the need to strengthen the Eagles' squad in an attempt to maintain Premiership status. As mentioned previously, the side that gained promotion to the top flight had barely managed to scrape into the play-offs towards the end of April, and required major surgery if it was to prove successful in the higher division. That major surgery had included the purchase of new, Premier-class players commanding big transfer fees and similar wages, but also instigated something of a purge of the professional staff who, it was deemed, were not cut out for the self-proclaimed 'hardest league in the world'.

In effect, while the Lombardos, Warhursts and Padovanos made the headlines, there was a simultaneous and constant stream of players leaving Selhurst Park, often much to the disappointment of the Palace faithful. No more Carl 'goal machine' Veart — sold to Millwall for £100,000. No more 'Ooh, aah' George Ndah — transferred to Swindon Town for £350,000. Farewell to Gareth 'hot head' Davies — Reading got their man for £175,000. Less well-known names like Jason Harris and Dean Wordsworth were also released, to Orient and Stevenage respectably. Added to the sale of Hopkin, Houghton and Day, it is easy to see that many of the links with the side Dave Bassett had tipped for greatness had already been lost.

In their place, Palace continued to dabble in the Italian market: Ivano Bonetti came and went; Sean Sogliano and Luca Luzardi were rejected after a trial; later Patrizio Billio would earn a week-by-week contract. However, while it was obvious that the majority of those released would not feature in a first choice Premiership starting line-up, it was hard not to feel a pang of frustration as the team, built up after the traumas of 1994/95, was systematically dismantled. It was an odd feeling. Alan Smith's promotion winners had been broken up having suffered relegation a year later. Reluctantly, that made sense, and yet here was another successful Eagles' side being dismembered for very different reasons, and the old feelings of those released coming back to haunt us persisted right up to the most controversial sale — that of Dougie Freedman.

Freedman had been something of a hero at Selhurst Park in his first year and a half at the Club. In truth, there had been so few bright spots until Christmas of the 1995 campaign, he had been the one shining light in an otherwise dismal return to the Endsleigh League. Subsequently, he became the inspiration for Bassett's promotion push, scoring goals for fun and running amok against the sub-standard defences of Southend, Grimsby and (sorry Eric Young) Wolves. Although strangely subdued on the bigger stage at Wembley, Dougie had continued his sharp-shooting exploits in the goal-bonanza at the start of the 1996/97 season, matching David Hopkin and Bruce Dyer strike for strike, as Palace challenged Bolton at the top of the Football League.

Then things had changed. A fine individual goal at Burnden Park heralded a barren spell, both for the Scottish under-21 star and the Club in general. It wasn't until the defeat at Root's Hall in January that Freedman scored again and, by the time Wolves returned to Selhurst Park for the first leg of the play-offs, the Scotsman was not even in the starting eleven. His failure to make an impact was translated as 'laziness' on the terraces, although it was the old Dougie Freedman whose magnificent late brace practically guaranteed the Palace another trip to Wembley.

Rob Ellis recollects Dougie's impact: 'Freedman had no expectations to live up to when he arrived from Barnet, but he had two very good seasons to start off his Palace career. During that time, the fans began pinning their hopes on him and, when things started to falter a bit, people took that as a sign of a lack of effort on his part. Having established some kind of expectation, he did fall short of this later on. Then again, people have got to understand that it gets more difficult, particularly in a higher division'.

In the Scotsman's defence, he had had little opportunity to establish himself as a Premiership player since the start of the season. Initially banned, he subsequently found himself behind Warhurst, Dyer and Shipperley in the pecking order, despite the fact that Coppell's side was never prolific in front of goal. Indeed, they played their most attractive attacking football with Freedman in the line-up for the first 45 minutes against Bolton in September. Ultimately, Dougie continued to warm the bench, only showing flashes of his talent when called upon. How could a player who so convincingly out-thought, out-paced and out-skilled England's Gary Neville at Old Trafford not perform more consistently? Even so, few people actually envisaged Freedman being sold.

By mid-October, however, the plot had thickened. Freedman's contract was to expire in the summer of 1998 and, with the player's demands some distance from the Club's offer, the spectre of Bosman was looming large on the horizon. A frustrated Coppell was forced to face the reality of the situation. 'I had a chat with Dougie's agent after the last discussions about his contract had broken down and I said that the best thing to do in the light of us not being able to agree a new deal is to see if there's any reaction to him being available,' reflected the Palace boss. 'He came back and mentioned that Wolves had shown an interest.'

The irony of the situation was lost on no-one, and would indeed become more bizarre as the transfer progressed. Here was Dougie Freedman, bane of the Wolves, preparing to jump ship and sign for the Molineux outfit. Was McGhee simply trying to buy as many of the players who had denied him promotion in the past as possible and therefore ensure that the Midlands' club would be elevated this time around? Who knows? The deal eventually struck involved Jamie Smith, another scorer from the play-off clashes, moving south in direct exchange for Freedman and Kevin Muscat, whose own first team place would have come under threat by Smith's arrival. The protracted nature of the negotiations had allowed Freedman to enjoy one match on loan at Wolves — he duly opened his scoring account at Molineux by netting the club's opening goal in a 3-1 win over Swindon Town. To make matters worse in the coming months, as Palace struggled pitifully to prise open opposition defences, a quick flick to *Teletext* would regularly reveal 'Freedman' and 'Muscat' among the Wolves' scorers.

'I've said all along, and people seem to disbelieve me, but I wanted Dougie to stay,' moaned Coppell. 'I would still like Dougie at this club. But I work for an employer who's financially keen on running a business and I can't ignore the fact that we'd have got nothing for him in the end. Dougie was suggesting more and more that he'd wait until the end of his contract and walk away. The counter argument to that deal is that we might be getting something for the players now, but we could end up losing our Premiership status. Time will tell whether it was a good decision or not, but I honestly don't think it will be critical to our survival.'

With Freedman gone, Palace were linked again with a succession of wildly unrealistic transfer targets — all of which seem to have had some thread of truth behind them. Paul Gascoigne was sounded out ('the initial response was favourable,' according to the Palace manager), as was 'Beppe' Signori of Lazio while, on the domestic front, Dele Adebola appeared to be constantly on the brink of joining the Club from Crewe Alexandra. All came to nothing. Then came renewed speculation linking Juventus' Michele Padovano with a big money move to England, with Palace and Middlesbrough in the running to secure his signature. Ron Noades visited Turin and watched the player and, despite Bryan Robson's assertion that a deal was as good as done, the Italian international opted to rejoin forces with his former team-mate Attilio Lombardo at Selhurst Park in preference to a switch to the North-East.

Perhaps the allegations of a £150,000 agent 'bung' convinced the Teesiders to pull the plug on their proposed deal. Then again, maybe it was Padovano's description of Middlesbrough being a 'horrible town' that swayed their decision. As it was, the Italian took to the field at White Hart Lane to rapturous applause from Palace's travelling fans, applause that was repeated when he was stretchered off again eleven minutes from time.

In the press conference after the 'Spurs' triumph, a satisfied Coppell, at ease with the world, enthused about his new signing. 'At one stage it looked as though a deal was beyond us but, given our heightened awareness of being desperate to stay in the Premiership, we thought we'd go ahead. The bottom line is that he is a very good player.'

Whatever the 'Goalfinger's' overall impact on the field for Crystal Palace Football Club, he inadvertently played a major role in the Club's progressive development. The Italian's £1.71 million arrival and subsequent wages were largely financed by money injected into the Club by Mark Goldberg. Goldberg had signed an agreement to pay £3 million to have the opportunity to purchase his shareholding of the club from Ron Noades — an offer he had until 25 February 1998 to take up. If the total £30 million purchase could not be made, the £3 million would automatically become a 10 per cent shareholding in the Club, with Noades retaining his overall majority control. 'In effect,' wrote the Chairman in the match day programme, 'I am using Mark's option money to purchase the player which I am of the opinion Crystal Palace need at the present time.'

It was widely understood that Goldberg had envisaged buying his 'beloved' Club at some point in the future. Noades, too, had indicated that he had rejected two bids believed to be in the region of £25 million for the

Club — both from undisclosed sources. Yet Noades cared as passionately for Palace as anyone and the deal which was eventually struck was done with a certain reluctance by the Eagles' owner of seventeen years.

'I don't want to sell,' he told *Eagles* magazine in December. 'I announced in the summer that I was going to sell 10 per cent of the Club in order to raise more money to spend in the transfer market. Subsequently, I had to add a few juicy bits to the offer so, in order to secure the deal for 10 per cent and the money for Padovano, I've had to include an option on the sale of my shares. That's not something I wanted to do, but on the other hand it's also pitched at a level where perhaps the offer might not be accepted. I'm gambling with the ownership of the Club, for the benefit of Palace.'

With the benefit of hindsight, it seems incredible that Padovano — who would not feature for a full ninety minutes at any stage all season — was considered to be worth this much. It seems crazier still when one considers that Freedman had been sold, and that an almost identical fee to that of the Italian's had been spent on Itzik Zohar, who continued to warrant no more than a place in Steve Kember's reserve side.

Still, Noades appeared to be onto a winner regardless of whether the purchase deadline was met or not. Of course, all the supporters knew of Noades' prowess as a businessman, so this should have come as no surprise. He continued: 'Mark's been keeping on about wanting to buy the Club for about 12 months and, if he can bring more financial clout in, I may even stay on and enjoy it more. I've agreed to stay on for a minimum period anyway [twelve months].

'When I bought Palace I had to put eight people together and, to a certain extent, he'll have to do the same. The press have made Mark into a multi-millionaire but he isn't - he's got 23 per cent of a £100 million company and it's all in shares, so where's the dough? He'd have to bring in, I would think, at least two other people. After all, if Mark wants to buy my shares, that doesn't provide any money for Crystal Palace. It's only what he's got left over once he's done that which gives us any more financial clout than we had before.'

Goldberg, for his part, maintained his desire to work alongside Steve Coppell and Noades in an effort to realise all three parties' goals. 'I believe I can help bring sufficient funding to develop the stadium and, most importantly, develop the team further to secure our Premiership status,' he told *Clubcall*. 'I am looking to carry on developing the Football Club with Ron Noades as a team. I'm really excited to be involved and I hope that I can be an asset to the Club as a whole.'

Integral to the team's plans for the future appeared to be the construction of a new Main Stand at Selhurst Park, ideally stretching right around the ground like a mini Wembley Stadium. Just like the scaled down model inside the directors' entrance, the Club's proposals had been gathering dust at Taberner House for some time, with the Council reluctant to realise

Noades' ultimate ambition of a 42,000 all-seater stadium, the gates from which would provide Palace with the funds to challenge for future domestic honours. 'To a certain extent we missed the boat here because the local authority became socialist for the first time in 100 years. I had a lot of new local councillors that suddenly started feeling that they were representing 24 votes around the corner and became big-time Charlies.' Suffice to say, Noades and the Council hadn't really struck it off.

It was plain to see that, if Palace were to progress to the next stage of their development, a larger stadium would be necessary to house (and fund) their greater ambitions. The Council was the first barrier to this goal, closely followed by a need to generate £8 million to build the new stand. If Mark Goldberg and his backers could supply this revenue, then the dream could become a reality. However, if he couldn't, Noades would not be complaining: 'We'd just have to carry on, beavering away like we've done for the last 17 years, building things slowly. It upsets the supporters, because they think we should do this, that and the other and go out and spend money we haven't got. But we built one stand and we'll build the next one as well.'

From the Chairman's comments, it did not take a genius to work out that he was not at all keen on selling the Club he had systematically re-built from scratch since 1981. Similarly, it appears that he did not anticipate Goldberg being able to finance a £30 million purchase prior to the February deadline. In essence, the Club had been able to finance Padovano's transfer, and not much else had happened. True, Juventus seemed keen to set up a kind of 'understanding' between the two clubs, continuing the relationship which had developed over the Lombardo and Padovano deals and which potentially might help Goldberg raise the necessary funds, but that was it. Noades was still very much in control and had no real intention of relinquishing his grip.

What he could not control was the sudden explosion in the media suggesting the Club was on the verge of a multi-million takeover. Various reports alleged that the deal was as good as done, had already been completed or was simply awaiting the go-ahead from Turin! Mark Goldberg, the press's 'chairman elect', was suddenly thrust into the limelight alongside his five-year plan, which would see Palace competing with the best in a Selhurst Park super-stadium. Of course, Noades' and Goldberg's plans were practically identical — consolidation in the Premiership, stadium redevelopment, European qualification, total domination of all football in this country for at least thirty years. They were the same dreams as any football chairman or ambitious director in the country harbours. Instead, the press scented a bloody boardroom split which could jeopardise the Club's chances of survival and considerably unsettle its players.

The problem was that once the press had initiated these stories, they were inevitably going to persist with them until the February deadline had been met, passed or scrapped, regardless of who was in charge of the Club. Overnight, Palace went from being everyone's favourite away-day specialists to 'that club wrecked by internal strife and boardroom battles', a club where back-stabbers flourished and personalities clashed behind the scenes. Whether this was true or not didn't really matter. Mark Goldberg and Ron Noades had never voiced a public disagreement, and yet now everyone assumed they hated each other.

Of course, this state of limbo would be less damaging as long as results on the field continued successful. There was no reason to suggest things might degenerate — Padovano and Smith had recently arrived, Warhurst was back after a spell on the sidelines, Shipperley couldn't stop scoring. All knew how much depended on Palace staying in the Premiership above all else. It was with all this hanging over them that the Eagles were hurled into an injury crisis from which they never truly recovered.

5 - December

ZOHAR NOT SO GOOD
The Guardian, 27 December, 1997

While the takeover saga rumbled on in the background, attention returned to the small matter of the Premiership campaign and something of a fixture backlog over the Festive Season. Steve Coppell's side faced six league clashes over December, including the rescheduled trip to the Bolyn Ground — West Ham's infamous 'Stadium of No Light' — where Eyal Berkovic made a mockery of the Eagles' impressive away record. A draw at Filbert Street — where Uriah Rennie ensured the visitors would be up against it by sending off Marc Edworthy for 'running in a threatening manner' and then allowed Muzzy Izzet to re-enter play at his leisure to curl home the equaliser — and a stroll for Liverpool at Selhurst Park followed, before a creditable point was taken from Pride Park, Derby.

So then to the final home clash of the calendar year: Crystal Palace versus Southampton at Selhurst Park. The whole memory sends shivers down the spine. Dave Jones had been through some rough times since succeeding Graeme Souness at the Saints' helm over the summer. Indeed, the knives were very much out and in the process of being sharpened for the former Morecambe and Stockport County boss when his new charges recorded only four points from their first nine Premiership outings. However, astute forays into the transfer market for experienced professionals worked wonders as David Hirst (a £2 million buy from Sheffield Wednesday), Carlton Palmer (£1.5 million from Leeds United) and Kevin Richardson (£500,000 from Coventry City — why do Palace never buy players like them?) galvanised those around them and inspired a run of four wins in five outings. Kevin Davies, a parting gift from Souness prior to his resignation, had made more of an impact than Michael Owen by early December and had not looked back since netting the only goal of the game at the Dell against Palace in August.

The match, then, represented no easy pickings for Coppell's Eagles, even if everyone realised that, on paper, this was our best chance of a Selhurst win since Bolton had left with a point in September. It could all have been so different. Dyer hit the inside of a post with a scuffed effort, while Shipperley went agonisingly close to opening the scoring against his former club. With six minutes remaining before the break, Carlton Palmer strode off down the right hand side — a threatening Star Wars Imperial Scout Walker surrounded by the home side's panicky ewok midfielders, buzzing around him in a nerve-fuelled frenzy. The former England international found his way blocked, played the ball back to Jason Dodd, who sent an angled ball into the Palace area. If the video could have been paused at that point, most home fans would have been relieved to have seen Matthew Le Tissier idly musing over the meaning of life on the left-hand side of the area. There was no danger of the ball reaching him, so there was no danger of Southampton scoring.

Wrong. The way Palace's luck was slipping away should have prepared all for Matthew Oakley's stunning volley on the turn. It obviously hadn't prepared Kevin Miller, who could only stand rooted to the spot in amazement, as the ball crashed against the underside of the crossbar and in. Just as against Newcastle and Liverpool, Palace trailed to a goal scored just before the break. The second-half performance merited an equaliser, which duly arrived courtesy of Shipperley's fine anticipation at the far post. Then came the moment of truth. With the clock showing 78 minutes, Bruce Dyer was felled inside the area — by no means a clear-cut penalty — and the referee pointed to the spot. Here was a home win being handed to the Eagles on a plate...

In hindsight, that last paragraph should stand corrected. The moment of truth had actually come about five minutes earlier, when Neil Shipperley, only just back from a groin injury, had suffered a recurrence and was promptly substituted to warm, appreciative applause. Enter Itzik Zohar, Palace's Israeli star, an international with class, composure and, supposedly, a lethal delivery from set pieces. Lethal for whom had as yet remained a mystery. The rest, as they say, is history.

The formalities of Zohar's arrival at Palace in July had been hugely overshadowed by the signing of Attilio Lombardo. The Israeli, originally of Maccabi Tel Aviv but ultimately purchased from Belgium's Royal Antwerp, had impressed on the Club's pre-season tour of Finland, where he had netted the only goal of the game against Oulu. (They're a good side, that Oulu.) Rumours abounded that he was the Israeli national captain, just as Eyal Berkovic, Ronny Rosenthal and David Amsalem were as well. How does the Israel side actually work? Do they take it in turns to skipper the team so that their collective curriculum vitae will attract more scouts? Regardless of the numerous trialists who enjoyed spells at Mitcham under the eyes of Coppell, Lewington & Co, he appeared to fit the (wage) bill and his signature subsequently commanded a fee of £1.2 million.

Having put pen to paper, notably in the period of doubt as to whether Lombardo would be making the move to London, the 26-year-old declared that his legs were 'full of fire'. Some might argue that this was another reason to take a longer look at him before forking out such a substantial fee. At this stage, Itzik presumably thought he had been bought to replace David Hopkin. His logic would have made some sense. After all, the Eagles had not as yet purchased a creative midfielder, and a club the size of Crystal Palace does not spend £1.2 million on a player never likely to be a first choice in the side (Gabbiadini and Taylor aside, that is). Reports on his early progress were encouraging, with the local press stressing what a promising young prospect the Israeli was (at 26?), and Coppell went on record saying that he was the best passer at the Club, even once Lombardo had arrived.

Worryingly, however, Zohar was never given a starting role to utilise these famed passing abilities until injury had bitten so deep into the squad that there was no alternative. This said a lot. Admittedly, he had been forced to wait for a work permit, and had then suffered a minor ankle injury which prevented him from training. Once fit again, he had come off the bench for his debut against Chelsea at Selhurst Park, had featured in both the Hull City catastrophes and had experienced fifteen minutes at Old Trafford in October.

'It was a dream trip for me. Everything you have seen on television and read about in newspapers and all the things that other players tell you about Old Trafford and Manchester United were suddenly there before my own eyes,' he sighed shortly after that 2-0 defeat. 'It was something really huge, starting with the immense crowds on the streets as we travelled towards the ground. The atmosphere in the dressing rooms was very different and then, of course, to play in that impressive stadium must be every player's dream. I have now done all that.'

It may sound harsh, but everything Itzik gushed seemed to be another extract from a passing tourist's journal — 'Itzik Does England' so to speak. 'I've got many friends in London and remember there are already a few other Israeli players here such as Ronny (Rosenthal) and Eyal (Berkovic). I also have a lot of friends who have studied here and I used to come to London for a holiday every Christmas. I would see my friends and watch some football matches, including Crystal Palace.' Hmmm...

Itzik's best performance for Palace, including numerous outings in the reserve side, came against Newcastle United when he replaced the injured Andy Roberts for the last half hour. The Geordies had controlled the game impressively, having taken the lead through Ketsbaia, but Zohar was at least prepared to keep possession and play the simple pass. His display was more intelligent than inspiring, but he did set up Shipperley's consolation and earned himself a starting place against West Ham United. Perhaps drawing direct comparison with Berkovic in that game further damaged his confidence — he looked out of his depth, sluggish and was easily hassled off the ball whenever he found himself with it at his feet. It was back to the drawing board.

By the time he replaced Shipperley against the Saints, Zohar was a marked man, desperately needing to pull off one piece of magic, one scrap of comfort to endear him to the doubting Selhurst faithful. He was no longer an automatic replacement in midfield, but was being employed to fill any attacking void left by injury or suspension, starting at Derby as an out-and-out striker, which he patently could never be. Furthermore, even his team-mates seemed to question his ability. He had been training with Steve Kember and the reserves for long periods and maybe felt ostracised from the first team. Therefore, when Dyer was tripped in front of the Holmesdale, Zohar realised it was do or die. Score the penalty and instantly become the favourite who ended the home drought; miss it and confirm his lowly status as an expensive misfit, an outcast with no long-term future at the Club.

If ever one kick could play such a significant role in deciding a player's career in English football, this was it — at least only if you can describe the nervous, poorly directed and agonisingly weak attempt to beat Paul Jones as a 'kick'. Once the incredible frustration of another two points thrown away had been taken out on the cat, you had to feel sorry for Zohar. There could not have been a friendly face inside Selhurst Park as he trudged back to the dressing room after the game, and yet any sympathy going his way was wiped out by the events of the ensuing week.

Granted permission to return to Israel for New Year, presumably to recover mentally from the penalty incident, Zohar decided to employ his time 'away from football' playing for another of his former clubs, Maccabi Haifa, in a friendly with AC Milan. The Palace management was flabbergasted to hear this news, especially when a scratch Palace side, minus the 'psychologically scarred' Zohar, had just taken on Blackburn Rovers at Ewood Park with few striking or midfield options. It is unlikely that the Israeli's presence would have made any difference at all in the North West to the 2-2 scoreline, but no permission had been granted for the 26-year-old to turn out back in Tel Aviv. Perhaps he decided that he needed to restore his confidence with one of his fabled commanding and creative midfield displays against the Milanese giants. If that was the case, then he failed miserably and compounded his misdemeanour by missing another penalty. Feel sorry for Zohar? There could not have been a friendly face inside the Maccabi Haifa stadium as he trudged back to the dressing room after the game...

While the player wallowed in his depression, debate raged in South London as to why he and not Bruce Dyer had taken the penalty. The management insisted that Bruce's ankle injury would have prevented him from mustering up the sufficient power to beat Jones — a line apparently maintained by the player himself, although anyone who had seen Bruce's penalty at Goodison Park would realise that power is less important than placement in his penalty style.

'That was blatantly a cover up,' insists *Eagle Eye*'s Neil Witheroe. 'Everyone in the ground could see that Zohar and Dyer were arguing as to who should take the kick. Bruce wanted to take it, but Zohar walked up to him and took the ball from him. Then he went and tapped it back to the 'keeper. As soon as he'd missed, you could see the fury in the Palace players' eyes. That was it for him.'

Coppell's programme notes quickly skimmed over the Club's subsequent release of the player at a loss of £1.2 million: 'Itzik never really settled here and was unfortunate to miss that penalty against Southampton recently.' In fact, Coppell and Ray Lewington took direct responsibility for the purchase of the player, as Chairman Ron Noades reminded everyone later in the season, drawing a depressing curtain across the whole affair. He had come highly recommended, but had already experienced two spells with European clubs which had been curtailed within a season to allow him to return to Israel. The writing had been very much on the wall — Royal Antwerp had loaned him back to Beitar Jerusalem for the entire 1996/97 season after he had 'failed to settle' in Belgian football. Yes, that'll be the fast and furious world of Belgian football!

On the playing side, how he had fallen through the net of his trial at the Club remains a mystery. As Paul Romain put it so strongly in the match day programme, discussing Zohar's British sojourn: 'Sadly, having Itzik Zohar on trial during the summer wasn't apparently sufficient for us to spot that he was completely useless.'

Romain cited the Israeli's 'inability to move above a snail's pace' as a contributory factor in his failure to impress in the Premiership. He undoubtedly had some talent, of which we had seen only brief glimpses, but he had utterly failed to adapt to the British game. In short, he was no Berkovic. Unfortunately, while Zohar had gone, so had Palace's prospects of recording a home triumph before the turn of the New Year.

Neil Shipperley's substitution against Southampton, which had pre-empted the whole Zohar firing squad scenario, was just one incidence of a winter injury jinx which threatened to single-handedly drag Palace into the relegation zone. Ultimately, it did just that. Gary Sadler, the Club physio, found the doors to his treatment room busier than the Selhurst Park turnstiles on a Wimbledon 'home' afternoon as the knocks, bruises, strains, pulls, hernias and tears mounted up. A newly promoted outfit is expected to find life at a higher level hard enough without all this worry.

Initially, Palace had been relatively fortunate on the injury front. Apart from Zohar's ankle knock, which hardly constituted a major blow to the Club's chances, the only serious injury had befallen David Tuttle, whose (relatively) impressive start to the season had been abruptly halted by his broken ankle against Wimbledon. While Tutts' absence was a blow, however, the signings of Emblen and Smith, allowing Edworthy to revert to a centre-back role, and the emergence of Hreidarsson appeared to cover his loss. Warhurst had missed a few games through hamstring problems, but it wasn't until Attilio Lombardo suffered a similar fate with the *Azzurri* in Rome that the squad began to look relatively threadbare. The ship soon began to appear rudderless without two of its more seasoned campaigners on board.

'Palace had bought well in pre-season, and had certainly bought enough,' stressed supporter Rob Ellis. 'The problem was that all the experienced men brought in were injury prone. Everyone knew that was why Warhurst had not established himself at Blackburn, and Attilio had been injured for long periods at Juventus. I suppose that's why they commanded such relatively small transfer fees. There was always a risk that they might break down again, and in December that started to happen.'

When one adds to this duo the name of Neil Emblen — a regular in the Molineux rehabilitation room and, regretfully, at Mitcham too — then, for long periods, Palace had a combined fee of £5.1 million consigned to the treatment room rather than on the pitch. As Ellis pointed out, however, the management would have realised the likelihood of such a phenomenon when all three were purchased in the summer. The crisis was compounded further when all the attacking players at the Club simultaneously fell to pieces, leaving Sadler to patch them up as well as he could to provide Coppell with even the most basic front-line. Why the injuries only seemed to strike down the forwards was a mystery: Shipperley's scoring streak was curtailed by groin and hernia problems; Dyer was veritably assaulted by Alessandro Pistone's reckless challenge (uncarded of course) and was never truly fit again; Leon McKenzie had to return from a loan spell at Fulham with various ailments; and even youth teamer Clinton Morrison's shoulder kept popping out of its socket as the youngster followed the lead set by his senior counterparts.

Perhaps the worst injury problems beset the other big-name Italian on the Eagles' books, Michele Padovano. The former Juventus marksman had not completed a full game for his new Club, netting only once along the way, when he was withdrawn against Liverpool with a hamstring problem after his best 45 minutes yet. Three months later, he took to the field at St James' Park having recovered from this hamstring pull, a calf strain and a bout of 'flu, but was still unable to last a full ninety minutes as the season nose-dived into the first division.

'Although I hadn't heard all that much about him before he signed, Padovano looked a class act at Leicester and was unlucky to be substituted,' recollects Wags of *One More Point*. 'Once Edworthy had been sent off, though, they had to do something, so they sacrificed him. He looked good at home to Liverpool as well, but that was that. From then on, he never looked up for it.'

Padovano's arrival had greater repercussions for the Club. However, he had as yet failed to deliver on the pitch. He appears to be a very different player from his fellow countryman and Juve team-mate, Lombardo — especially 'up top' (and we're not talking intelligence here). Sitting in the weights area waiting to interview Steve Coppell in late November, my question preparation was interrupted by the Club's translator, Dario Magri, who scuttled into the room and eagerly surveyed the impressive array of fitness machinery. Was he about to make use of the facilities now that the players had departed? No, instead he appeared to be looking for something and, having focused on one of the high-tech electronic treadmills, he looked somewhat relieved. Rather than starting the machine up, however, he proceeded to unplug it from the wall before wandering off, calling out for Michele. The Italian appeared moments later and saw the lead disconnected from the wall. Ah, the true professionalism of the Italian footballer. In an effort to adapt to the physical, non-stop nature of the British game, Michele must be about to undertake some out-of-hours training. Wrong again. Without a moment's hesitation, the Italian plugged his hairdrier into the socket and began drying his flowing locks. Palace had obviously come up in the world.

Unfortunately, it seemed at times as if drying his hair was all Padovano ever did in the treatment room — or perhaps I am being unreasonable and unfair. Whatever did happen behind the scenes, most of it seemed to occur back in Turin where Lombardo and Padovano were sent to recuperate amidst the splendour of Juve's fitness facilities.

Sadler explained the Club's decision to let them return home: 'It was better for them to receive treatment in Italy rather than have to wait their turn here, and I'm sure they benefited psychologically. Both lads have played at the top level and look after themselves well, and they are thoroughly professional. If they have a slight injury, they make it known, but we are hopeful that the next time they pull on a Palace shirt they will be fit once more to resume our Premiership campaign.' Unfortunately for Palace, the two Italian stars would not be seen again until March, by which time the Eagles' fate was as good as sealed.

Still, with Lombardo and Padovano back in Turin, at least there was room on the treatment table for Paul Warhurst, who suffered a stress fracture of the leg in the lead up to the FA Cup third round tie with Scunthorpe United in the New Year. Similarly, Jamie Smith needed attention to his Achilles injury, picked up originally at West Ham, while Andy Roberts and Simon Rodger were also booked in for check-ups in Sadler's crisis clinic. Poor Coppell and Lewington were at a loss. The squad, which had looked so convincing on paper in mid-November, had been decimated, and players not normally expected to feature were suddenly on the verge of the first team. This had been a potential problem in November — Rory Ginty's number 34 shirt had to be taken to White Hart Lane late in the day by someone on work experience at the Club when the Irishman suddenly fell into line for a debut — but was now a reality over the Festive Season. Darren Pitcher, the extent of whose match practice had been a single reserve team fixture since suffering cruciate knee ligament damage in September 1996, and who would retire from the professional game within three months, found himself on the bench at Ewood Park. Ginty started his second successive Premiership match the same afternoon.

At the turn of the year, players, management and supporters reflected on the Club's progress towards Premiership safety. The Eagles, as yet without a home win, were still three places and three points above the relegation zone, with 23 points from 21 games. Chairman Ron reflected the mood around Selhurst Park: 'We've had a spate of injuries recently which has left us without our main strikers. If we can overcome the injury problems which we've had, we'll be alright. I am convinced that we will give a good account of ourselves in the Premier League if we can pick our best side.' As 'ifs' go, that was quite a substantial one...

6 - January & February

EVERYONE THRASHES THEM
Wimbledon manager, Joe Kinnear

January and February carried the potential to make or break the whole season. Six Premiership fixtures, four of them at Selhurst Park, and the FA Cup, would demonstrate the relevance of the Eagles' run-in. Furthermore, the deadline was nearing for Mark Goldberg's proposed £30 million takeover at the end of February. These could be momentous months.

In the event, they were disastrous. The scene was set in the cup-tie against Third Division Scunthorpe United, when high winds caused the closure of the Upper Tier of the Holmesdale practically on the stroke of kick-off. While chaos reigned at that end of the ground — with season ticket holders wandering around in the pouring rain like lost sheep, increasingly irate at not having seats from which to enjoy the cup game — a similar farce was played out on the pitch. Brian Laws' side hit the post, should have scored shortly afterwards and went in at half-time justifiably aggrieved at being behind to Neil Emblen's scuffed goal. The second half continued in much the same vein, with Emblen scoring a decisive second on the stroke of full-time while the wind howled around the stadium like a demented banshee. The management team must have suppressed similar screams as they watched their charges being outclassed by the Yorkshiremen, who were in the process of throwing away their chances of maintaining a promotion drive from the lowest division of the Football League.

Unfortunately, that win over Scunthorpe was as good as it got for a while. Dreadful defeats against fellow strugglers Everton and Barnsley followed, dragging Palace to within two points of the foot of the table. Suddenly, criticism of the team formation was rife and to blame for all the woes in the world. Ray Lewington was quick to respond: 'We played the same formation all last season and no-one complained, but now that we are not winning games everyone is blaming the system. It's simply nothing to do with the formation — it's the personnel.

'At the moment we are lacking creative players to break other teams down. This is reflected in our respective home and away records. Undoubtedly we miss David Hopkin most of all — he had the ability to make runs from deep, had two good feet, an excellent touch and could hit the target. He typifies the type of player who benefits from this style. Coupled with the lack of creative midfielders, our full-backs are too tentative at the moment which restricts our attacking options. On the other hand, what are the alternatives?'

As far as *Eagle Eye*'s Neil Witheroe is concerned, Lew had hit the nail right on the head. 'We had never replaced David Hopkin sufficiently,' he stresses. 'Okay, so we'd bought Lombardo who was an outstanding signing, but he made us change the whole method of the team. You can't blame the Italian, though. Hopkin was integral to the way Palace had played in gaining promotion, and the only effort to find a like-for-like player seemed to have been the purchase of Zohar, who was useless. That has to come down to a management failing.'

Increasingly, it became obvious that the team lying on Sadler's treatment table was better than the one out on the pitch. The problem was that the injury list showed little sign of easing. Witheroe continues: 'When we went up to Derby in December, I looked at the team we had out and thought to myself, "It can't get worse than this. We're going to get thrashed out there." We had players playing out of position, youth teamers being thrust into the starting line-up and no-one on the bench who could come on and change a game. As it was, that was practically the same team we were forced to play for the next three months. They didn't stand a chance. It's debatable whether we would have gone down without the injuries, but it certainly wouldn't have become so hopeless so soon.'

Victory over Leicester in the Cup papered over a few cracks and gave the media the novelty of a Palace home win against Premiership opposition. Bruce Dyer, a hat-trick hero that day, but increasingly erratic over the course of the season, was featured on the draw for the fifth round, along with the few lower league giant-killing managers remaining in the competition. That was it — Palace had been relegated to the role of 'giant-killers' with a home win against a poor Leicester City side. It was embarrassing.

It got worse. The recently signed Tomas Brolin was humiliated at home to Leeds United; Wimbledon ran riot in front of the SKY cameras with Carl Leaburn scoring twice (doubling his entire career tally); Arsenal reserves won easily at Highbury; and Coventry City became the latest recipients of the 'please score three times at Selhurst Park' invitation at the end of the month, which they accepted with relish. In the Cup, the Gunners eventually triumphed in a replay in South London against ten-man Palace, but at least Dyer scored in that game. It was the only goal the team mustered up in all six fixtures.

Of course, the injuries were primarily to blame. 'Without strikers you are impotent in this division,' bemoaned an increasingly crestfallen Coppell after the Wimbledon disaster. 'They had two centre-forwards on the bench, while we struggled to put two on the pitch.' One of those was the portly Brolin, whose initial reaction to being selected against Everton had been to crease up into a fit of hysterics.

The side was now at rock bottom and the strikers' injury jinx continued. Padovano was on course for a return against the Foxes, but suffered a calf strain 24 hours before kick-off. Coppell explained: 'We had him training for a week and then he went down on the Friday before the game. We do next to nothing on a Friday for that very reason. I've always said you can only do damage on a Friday. We did next to nothing and then he suddenly came down with a calf strain. So the injury has been very disappointing.' Even new players were not exempt. Former Carlisle striker Matt Jansen was given a run out in the reserves having joined for £2 million and lasted just ten minutes before hobbling from the field with a dead leg. This was ridiculous.

By far and away the most damaging injury loss, however, came not to a player, but to first team coach Ray Lewington who twisted his knee while conducting training at Streete Court and entered hospital for what was thought to be a routine operation to correct the problem. A month later, Lew had still to be discharged and was fighting for his life to stop the poison from his infected knee taking over his entire body. It was widely understood that Lew was the inspiration behind Palace's style of play — whether it had been under Dave Bassett or Steve Coppell, in the First Division or the Premiership. Without him, one of the most significant cogs in the management machine was missing and the strain on Coppell was greatly increased. Palace never really recovered from his absence.

So, on the pitch, things had gone from bad to worse. What, then, of the takeover which had been simmering away in the background since Padovano's arrival in late November? For much of the interim period, little had been said of the potential purchase of the Club. Either no-one believed Mark Goldberg could raise the required money, or perhaps he had got cold feet and decided, with the team plummeting towards oblivion, that the purchase was unwise by the deadline of 27 February. Yet, while the takeover was not on the tips of everyone's tongue, the personalities involved remained firmly in the headlines.

Both Noades and Goldberg continued to insist that they both had Crystal Palace's interests at heart, despite there being major differences in their respective ideologies — not least regarding transfer policy. Over January and February, as the injury crisis persisted, Palace bought, and were constantly linked with, a number of players. The list seemed endless: Marcus Bent, a 19-year-old striker from Brentford with a handful of goals to his name in a hatful of appearances for the West London outfit, had signed for £150,000; 20-year-old Matt Jansen had rejected Manchester United (threatening to compete in the Champions' League for 1998/99) in favour of a £2 million move to Palace (threatening to compete in the Nationwide League for 1998/99); the Club's transfer record had been broken to secure the services of French under-21 international Valérien Ismael for £2.75 million, and former Swedish star and Leeds misfit, Brolin, had joined until the end of the season on reported wages of £16,000 a week.

Then came the links. Tommy Johnson was lined up for a loan move from Celtic to ease the depleted strikeforce. Johnson might be remembered as much for vomiting through nerves on his Aston Villa debut as for his carrot-top hair-cut. He was a player with proven Premiership experience and an enviable goalscoring record, *ie:* exactly what Palace needed at the time. As it was, Johnson never signed, as FIFA officials had all left the office early for the weekend when the Club tried to tie up the loan deal! This doesn't happen on *Championship Manager 2*.

Italian Patrizio Billio regularly featured in the reserves while the Club worked out whether he'd ever actually played for AC Milan and therefore whether there was any real kudos in signing him. Another controversial foreigner, Sasa Curcic of Aston Villa, was the subject of a £1 million bid in February, but doubts remained as to whether the Yugoslav would be granted a work permit once the season had drawn to a close. As it happened, he then went into hospital to undergo an operation on his nose, before promptly marrying an English girl whom he'd met in a supermarket in Birmingham. Both these players would ultimately end the season at Selhurst Park.

Then there were Temuri Ketsbaia (one good game against Palace and he was a world beater), John Salako, Andy Goram, Leo Koswell (heard of him?) and, of course, Paul Gascoigne. The Rangers midfielder had been linked with Palace since *Clubcall* had picked up on a particularly speculative rumour that summer, but each time the stories had come to nothing. Now, though, Mark Goldberg waved the possible return of Terry Venables as bait at Gazza and, for one unforgettable day, it appeared English football's big fish had bitten. Trevor McDonald on *News at Ten* claimed Palace had agreed a fee with the Glasgow club, and that Gazza and his mentor, El Tel, would lead the Club to the promised land of mid-table security. 48 hours later, McDonald remained po-faced as he announced that the Geordie had signed for Middlesbrough in a £3.5 million deal. Perhaps Danny Baker had warned Gazza against a move to Selhurst Park. Who knows? Who cares?

'There was absolutely no way that Gascoigne was ever coming to Palace,' reflects Witheroe. 'Maybe if we had been mid-table, or at least with a points cushion between us and the relegation places, he might have considered it. But with us five points adrift at the bottom of the table, there was no chance.'

So we had Padovano, they had Gascoigne. Palace 1 Middlesbrough 1. The golden goal decider could have been Coventry's Dion Dublin, who had rejected a £16,000 a week new contract at Highfield Road, but common sense eventually prevailed in his case. Why leave a resurgent Coventry when the alternatives were Palace, Boro', Wimbledon and Leicester — amazingly the only other clubs reportedly taking an interest in him? He stayed and naturally scored at Selhurst at the end of February.

Each one of these players smacked of being either a Goldberg or a Noades buy. While both might have seen Jansen's immense potential (after all, if Manchester United wanted him, he must be good), Noades now returned to his 'buying for the future' philosophy. Marcus Bent had no experience of the top level — unlike Ndah, who had been sold — but was skilful and enthusiastic. The management admitted they had been reluctant to throw him immediately into the Premiership cauldron, but the attacking absentees forced their decision. Bent would do them proud as he visibly learnt from the disasters all around, and had become something of a crowd favourite by the end of the season.

Ismael, perhaps unfairly, had been expected to adjust immediately, having commanded such an immense transfer fee. Coppell later admitted that Ron Noades had been watching another Strasbourg player when the defender caught the chairman's eye. While he may have been unknown to the majority of Palace fans, he had played against Liverpool in the UEFA Cup earlier in the season, and had made a name for himself on the continent. Rob Ellis, for one, was no stranger to Ismael's talents: 'I knew something about him, having watched European football. I had heard him being touted amongst the French players as one of their best young central defenders. He was a very good signing, but one for the future and not what we needed in January.'

Unfortunately for Valérien, he was exposed to the Crazy Gang rather too early for comfort in his Palace career. Even Leaburn looked a world beater as the Frenchman stumbled around the area in a daze, the Dons scoring three times in the first twelve minutes of the second period. This didn't exactly endear Val to the Holmesdale End and he became inexorably linked with the season's new lowest point. He was young enough to recover and should still develop into a fine player — with or without Palace.

So, these were the Noades' signings, bought for a future which could either be in the Premiership or the First Division. They made good business sense, even if the money paid for the Frenchman seemed slightly excessive. Mark Goldberg, meanwhile, appeared to favour proven players who might, just might, inspire the side to win the odd game over the remainder of the campaign. Salako, Curcic, Gascoigne and Dublin were all 'big name' players, although arguably only the latter could have helped lift the Eagles away from the bottom three, and he was probably the unlikeliest of the quartet ever to join the Selhurst Park outfit.

With the Club apparently looking to monopolise the transfer market in a way unheard of since Barry Fry bought the entire population of Birmingham to play for the Blues, you couldn't help but wonder what Steve Coppell, and Ray Lewington from his hospital bed, thought about it all. It was almost as if the management would arrive at Mitcham each day wondering which new players would be changed and bibbed, ready for training and guidance. With his Chairmen playing each other off, and politics no doubt dictating who should be in the first team, Coppell's position seemed increasingly luckless.

Neil Emblen had given his impression of the situation when he'd signed for the Club back in August. 'I think it was Mark Goldberg who was instrumental in getting me to Palace, rather than Ron Noades, and possibly even over Steve Coppell's head,' he told *Eagles* magazine. 'When I spoke to Steve early on he did say that when Mark told him about me he'd reacted positively. But it may possibly have all been done in the wrong way. In truth, Steve and Ron may not even have wanted me in the first place. From day one, when I went in to see the manager, he implied that Mark had got me here and I wasn't necessarily guaranteed this or that. So from the very first minute I was like, "Ummm?"' His initial impression was later confirmed, when the Club accepted an offer from Wolves to buy back the defender at almost half the price. Added to the Zohar money, the princely sum of £2 million had been frittered away, the same price paid to secure a player of Matt Jansen's ability.

Ultimately, it didn't seem to matter whom the Club tried to buy — whether they bought to try and maintain their Premiership status with established, experienced international stars or in preparation for a season in Division One. Neither would have kept the Club in the top flight. The damage had already been done, thanks to the never-ending list of injuries, which only eased once the Eagles had made their roost uncomfortably on the lowest rung of the Premier League ladder. Instead, the transfer dealings suggested that each party in the takeover saga was attempting to convince the fans that his was the best way forward. It all added to the tension — on the pitch, in the stands and in the boardroom.

Whenever asked, Ron Noades had consistently asserted that he did not want to sell the Club. Furthermore, he did not think that Goldberg would ever be in a position to purchase it from him. That was until 25 February, 1998 - two days before the deadline he had imposed back in November. On the day Palace were preparing to take on Arsenal in an FA Cup fifth round replay, Ron consented in principle to hand over the reins. An initial sum of £10 million was to be paid as a deposit, with a further £20 million to be transferred to Noades in stages, eventually securing Goldberg 85 per cent of the Club's shares. If everything went to plan, Ron would hand over control in October, remaining as Chairman until then to allow Goldberg time to adjust to life as a football club supremo.

While three months had passed since the initial talk of a takeover bid, Noades' decision appeared to come as something of a surprise. Witheroe explains: 'At that point, it was on the cards that Goldberg might actually raise the money required, so Ron could no longer keep denying that he was going to sell the Club. There was always a veneer that Goldberg was a benevolent benefactor, but Noades could not keep insisting that the Club wasn't up for sale when, quite clearly, it was. It was damage limitation in his own eyes.'

Similarly, could Noades the businessman really look a gift horse in the mouth and reject a £30 million bid for a Club descending back into the First Division as quickly as it had risen? It seemed not.

The day was spent with Goldberg elaborating on his plans for the Club, outlining a new management set-up, a 40,000 all-seater super stadium, new signings and how relegation had never entered his mind. He toured the ground prior to kick-off, lord of all he surveyed, flirting with the television cameras who were present for the more mundane matter of a football match. He suggested that Terry Venables could be on the verge of a return to Selhurst Park (hence the Gazza links), while there was a new role for Steve Coppell within the football club: 'Steve has agreed to become Development Director of Football and I'm delighted that he is going to become very much part of my five-year plan to implement the right infrastructure to enable us to be competing in Europe within the next five years.'

After the Lord Mayor's Show came the football match, which Palace inevitably lost. All this put Coppell in an untenable position at the post-match press conference, a situation which, typically, he handled with great dignity and admirable tact. 'I am manager of the football club until the owner, whoever he is, tells me otherwise. At the moment, the owner of the Club is Ron Noades. The option of performing a different role other than that of manager, or leaving the Club, doesn't leave me with an option.

'I'm not jumping to any assumptions. I am manager of the Club and the players are looking for someone to give them direction. Leadership comes from the boss... I'm the boss. Without doubt I wish it was all settled today. But summer follows spring. I could mention swallows, but...'

In reality, Coppell's position at the helm had been tenuous since the turn of the year, at least in the eyes of the press. Gerry Francis, dismissed from White Hart Lane and a friend of Noades, had been tipped for a return to South London, but the Club refused to comment at the time. Coppell, however, was becoming increasingly irritated by the constant speculation: 'If Ron thinks Gerry can do a better job than me, I'd have no problem with that. I would happily go.' No smoke without fire...

'I have to say that there is no truth in that story at all,' replied Francis, who would no doubt have been attracted by the homely nature of the Club's lengthy injury list after his miserable spell at 'Spurs. 'It is well known that the Palace chairman is a friend of mine and some people are putting two and two together and making five, but the basic fact is that I don't feel ready to come back into the game just yet.'

Later in the year, after Palace had suffered the depressing drop back into the Football League, Noades revealed that a managerial change had been very much on the cards. He told *Eagles* magazine 'Gerry was coming, but then he realised if Mark took over and Terry Venables came in, he would be out. It was a pity because, had he come, I don't think we'd have gone down.'

Now though, Coppell was being forced to remain in charge while Goldberg (rather than Noades) sounded out his likely replacement, Terry Venables, who was still under contract to the Australian Football Association. This was all very unsatisfactory and rather messy. Noades was officially Chairman and in charge, but Goldberg was effectively taking the decisions for the Club's future. If ever a club could have two chairmen, this was it. Still no-one knew what was really going on.

To add to the confusion, the press concentrated on Goldberg's plans to sell 10 per cent of Crystal Palace to Juventus. It is not clear whose brainchild this venture was, as Noades had confirmed in November that preliminary discussions had been held with the Italian giants. 'There's an awful lot of cross-fertilisation going on at the moment,' he had stated. 'You've got Arsenal talking about investing in Cannes, and then there's people like Joe Lewis, who's invested in Rangers, AEK Athens... in fact four clubs, I believe.'

It appears that Goldberg had undertaken many of these discussions himself and was now anxious to achieve a permanent understanding with the *Serie A* side. 'When I first negotiated with Juventus, Roberto Battega showed an interest in us. I took advantage of that and, over the last few months, Roberto and myself have become friends and I am convinced, in fact there is no doubt, that they could be a great asset to Crystal Palace. I'm proud of the fact that I might be able to bring them into the party. Juventus will come on board as technical directors of football. They'll be looking to implement their model of success within Crystal Palace FC and they'll be re-investing their management fee on an annual basis into a 10 per cent shareholding in the Club, which shows a hell of a commitment on their part.'

The Juventus proposal was mouth-watering, but made little sense. It might have done if the Eagles were comfortably mid-table in the Premiership, but Palace were nose-diving alarmingly and, whenever the Juventus delegation had watched the Club, they had put the kiss of death on Coppell's players — Newcastle at home (1-2) and West Ham away (1-4) being cases in point. If their presence made the team perform like this, maybe Selhurst Park should remain a Juve-free zone (after all, no one had seen an Italian playing there since mid-December anyway). Indeed, their continued interest seemed incredible, given allegations in the Italian magazine, *Tutosport*, that the injured duo Attilio Lombardo and Michele Padovano had been highly critical of Palace's training facilities at Mitcham. Their alleged comments were picked up in a London newspaper which rubbed further salt into the Club's wounds — even if the misunderstanding appeared to centre on another mistranslation. To cap it all, Palace had their own pair of Ravanellis on top of everything else. However, both players quickly apologised for any embarrassment their comments might have caused.

'Those words were neither mine nor Padovano's,' insisted Lombardo. 'Some Italian reporters made up a bit of a story, then the English papers picked it up and made it worse. The last thing we would want to do is start back-stabbing the Club.' At least the story reminded Palace fans that both players were still at the Club, even if they spent most of their time back in Turin receiving treatment.

So February drew to a close with very little resolved. True, Mark Goldberg had taken another step towards purchasing the Club he had ardently followed for years, but the deal now looked as if it was going to drag on until October, increasing confusion and disharmony. Meanwhile, on the playing side, the Eagles' points tally had ground to an abrupt halt: 23 points from 26 games prior to Coventry's visit, and only Dyer's penalty against Everton to add to the 'goals for' column. It was all fairly desperate, particularly with one coach in hospital and most of the first team still undergoing treatment for the knocks and bruises suffered before Christmas. No-one seemed to know how to arrest the decline.

During an interview with Palace's Pete King on *Selhurst Six*, prior to kick-off at the match against Coventry City on 28 February, Ron Noades stressed that he was still very much the Chairman of Crystal Palace and that much could change in the coming months, especially if the instalments were not met. 'Chairmen', management and players alike insisted that the off-the-field confusion had not disrupted the team's concentration during matches; it could not be used as an excuse for the side's poor form and sudden plunge down the table. Before leaving to take his seat in the Directors' Box, Noades warned against Palace conceding an early goal against the rampant Sky Blues, who were in the midst of a similar record-breaking sequence, although of the more successful kind. Early concessions had occurred in mid-week against Arsenal and also against Leeds and Everton over the past two months. All agreed: keep it solid for the first twenty minutes, and maybe that elusive first home win would materialise at last.

47 seconds into the match, Dean Gordon shinned an attempted clearance and the ball fell to Paul Telfer just outside the six-yard box. His shot nestled inside the far corner. Palace 0 Coventry 1. Welcome to the 'three goals club', Gordon Strachan.

7 - March

...BEING RUN OVER BY A LORRY!

Attilio Lombardo on his appointment as player/coach, 13 March, 1998

If January and February had suggested Crystal Palace Football Club was descending into a state of near anarchy, then nothing had prepared us for the mayhem that was March. The Coventry catastrophe had sent the Eagles to the foot of the Premiership table for the first time and few believed that the team, with six straight league defeats behind them, could claw their way out of the mire. The takeover was apparently going ahead, although not until October, by which time it seemed likely that Palace would be in the midst of a Nationwide League campaign in a bid to regain their top division status. Things, in short, looked grim and a trip to Stamford Bridge was hardly likely to provoke a revival in the team's fortunes.

Newspaper talk prior to the game in West London had centred on Terry Venables taking over as manager, in a bid to stave off relegation. He was reportedly set to buy a stake in the Club, alongside fellow investors Juventus, offered by Mark Goldberg as something of a carrot to tempt the former England manager back for a second stint at Selhurst Park. 'Terry Venables is, in my mind, the only man who can turn round the current lack of confidence,' Goldberg told the media. 'I have studied Terry's history quite carefully and I am convinced that I can work with him. He won't be involved in any other aspect of running the Club, but that does not mean I can't offer him a share option scheme for when we go public in five years' time.'

Goldberg met Venables on 2 March and discussed a five-year contract to manage the Club, allegedly worth in the region of £1.5 million. El Tel was set a deadline for the following Monday to take up the computer tycoon's offer as both men expressed their pleasure at the way the talks had progressed. A week later, however, Venables was in Spain and his decision was not as yet forthcoming. In his absence, Goldberg stated that no players would be brought into the Club without his prospective new manager's recommendation and all waited to hear the ex-Barcelona and 'Spurs boss's decision. The wall of silence persisted. The next thing the supporters knew was that Palace's Chairman-Elect had met with John Barnes, who was known to favour a break into management once his playing days were over. With Newcastle United spiralling down the table, some thought they already were.

In the meantime, it was confirmed that Juve were not permitted to own shares in Crystal Palace under Italian law. Instead, the *Serie A* leaders indicated that they were ready to reinvest the management fee and charge the Eagles for providing technical expertise, thus securing the ten per cent stake. While a deal had not as yet been struck, it seemed a possibility, but not with Palace bringing up the rear in the Premier League. Such stories gave the trip to Stamford Bridge even greater significance as Palace looked to rekindle their celebrated away form which, in truth, had deserted them since November.

How Steve Coppell was expected to motivate his players in the wake of such allegations, speculation and management mystery remained an enigma. Technically, he was still manager of Crystal Palace, working for Ron Noades, but he more than anyone must have been aware that the backroom scene was changing. Mark Goldberg's insistence that only El Tel could rescue the Club from its predicament hardly inspired much confidence in the Palace manager's ability to turn things around. With Venables tipped to take over before too long, and Coppell being moved upstairs into a new role, the former Manchester United winger found himself in as much of a state of limbo as the whole Club. Now he had the unenviable task of convincing his players that the clash with Vialli, Zola and friends would provide the perfect springboard towards an ascent of the table. In the process, he may as well have pointed out that bacon did have strong aerodynamic capabilities, and that Lord Lucan had been spotted at Streete Court and was in line to make his debut at Villa Park on the following Saturday. The way things were going, anything was possible.

Amazingly, Chelsea were struggling, having lost four league games in a row and had suffered a slump to fifth (as slumps go, this did not constitute that much of a crisis) under Gianluca Vialli's management. However, the hangover from Ruud Guillit's dismissal had not extended to cup competitions, for interspersed among calamitous defeats at the hands of Leicester City and Aston Villa were impressive triumphs over Arsenal and Real Betis. They faced the prospect of two cup finals before the end of the season, and could still reassert themselves to claim a UEFA Cup spot by right if their league form improved. The prospect of a match against the basement club had Blues' players and supporters fairly champing at the bit.

So, Coppell and his squad made the short journey to the King's Road in hope rather than expectation. They were still without Ray Lewington, who remained confined to a hospital bed and whose role in the dug-out had been temporarily assumed by Brian Sparrow. Furthermore, the Club had decided to accept a surprise bid of £1.6 million for captain Andy Roberts two days earlier from Wimbledon and he had since joined the Crazy Gang. Chelsea's programme, while admirably up to date on the sudden transfer, was under the misconception that the £2.25 million signing from Millwall had been an integral member of the Eagles' back-line; 'The central pillars in recent weeks have been "Rhino" Roberts and the excellent man-marker Hreidarsson... But the surprising sale of Roberts to Wimbledon at the weekend poses plenty of questions without answers. How will Palace play? How will their players react?'

In all honesty, Roberts' form had been desperately disappointing for some time. He possessed neither the pace nor the skill to grace the midfield which Palace needed in the Premiership, and seemed increasingly better employed as a sweeper. Unfortunately, the Eagles had at least three other candidates for that position, forcing Andy into a midfield berth he never appeared to relish. Wags, of *One More Point*, was not unhappy to see him leave: 'He had not turned into the Premiership player we had all expected he would have and had suffered the curse of the captain's armband. Mind you, at that stage of the season, it didn't really matter who we sold. Anyone could have left and it really would not have made a jot of difference to the final outcome.'

Mark Goldberg pointed an accusatory finger at the Bosman Ruling in explaining the decision to let the captain 'jump ship'. 'Andy was coming to the end of his contract and could have left for nothing at the end of the season,' he stated. 'We have to look for a more inspiring captain.' For the Chelsea fixture, the armband was handed to Simon Rodger, who led the team out under the Stamford Bridge lights in front of a good-sized crowd of almost 32,000. Lambs to the slaughter...

Steve Coppell cut an awkward figure in the post-match press conference. He obviously did not want to be the centre of attention after a night of footballing humiliation and, for once, the predatory hacks seemed reluctant to crow over the team's rotting carcass by attacking a man whose hands were patently tied. At times, the silence was more than deafening.

[*Embarrassed pause*] 'Er, Steve. How much of this defeat was down to events off the pitch?'

'We were eleven strangers defensively. We were so fragile at the back it was unbelievable, but there are no excuses. You can't blame our rank bad defending on all this other stuff.'

[*Silence*]

'Well, gentlemen. Will that be all?'

[*Muttering*] 'Yes, thank you Steve.'

The sigh of relief when Gianluca Vialli strode confidently into the room to hail his side's 6-2 triumph appreciably broke the tension. The elation that had exuded from the Palace camp after the post-match comment at White Hart Lane in November seemed a very distant memory. A seventh successive defeat told its own story.

The Club's response to the mauling at the hands of Zola and Vialli was to call its own press conference at Mitcham two days later. It was expected that Terry Venables would be unveiled as the new Palace chief, with Coppell assuming his role as 'technical director of football' as Mark Goldberg had always favoured. The training area, where Padovano had dried his hair with such an air of nonchalance months previously, was now crammed with photographers, reporters and bemused youth team players anxious to force their way through the throng and seek solitude in the changing rooms beyond. As it transpired, the Club had yet another surprise up its sleeves.

As expected, Steve Coppell moved upstairs, taking advantage of the five-year contract offered by the Chairman-Elect, which granted him the security he had never enjoyed as a non-contract manager under Ron Noades. In his place, however, was not El Tel, but Attilio Lombardo, assuming temporary charge of team affairs presumably until Venables signed on the dotted line and returned to his old stamping ground. The change stunned the media and fans, particularly as Lombardo's English was by no means perfect, coupled with the fact that he had only returned from a three month injury lay-off as a substitute at Stamford Bridge two days earlier.

'It is a bold, massive step and a lot of people will look on it as foolish, but at least we are trying to be positive,' insisted Coppell, who took his place alongside Lombardo and Club interpreter Dario Magri at the conference. The latter, a restaurateur with no obvious football connections other than Ivano Bonetti being his cousin, had been employed initially to help Lombardo adjust to life in a new country. Incredibly, he would find himself screaming orders from the bench in front of the *Match of the Day* television cameras before the month was over. Only at Palace. Coppell continued: 'It might not work, but then everyone outside the Club thinks we are going down anyway. It's been a slow strangulation where we have been drifting down the league. It was time for a change in view of the fact that my position would be changing and we had in our midst a man who has as much respect and achievement as anyone in the game.'

This was all true. Lombardo had the respect of the players, the management and the supporters and Coppell's position had become increasingly untenable — whether down to player disenchantment or the changing of the guard in the boardroom did not matter. Significantly, Steve had lost his right-hand man with Ray Lewington's injury, and it had become increasingly evident that things could only get worse unless some kind of change was implemented, and fast. Still, Coppell had made a mockery of his 5-4 odds-on status with the bookies to be the first Premiership manager to lose his job. Messrs Pleat, Francis, Guillit and Little had all faced the wrath of Madame Guillotine well before Steve stepped aside in mid-March.

As for Lombardo, this was a new and unexpected challenge. He had watched with admiration as his great friend Vialli had taken up the reins offered to him by Ken Bates at Chelsea and, on being asked to do the same for Palace, had used his statutory 'one phone call' to seek the advice of his former Juve and Sampdoria team-mate before accepting the role.

'I had half an hour to make a decision and it felt like being run over by a lorry,' he, or rather Dario, told the massed ranks of paparazzi. 'I am looking forward to it, but my intention is not to remain as player-manager.

This is a temporary measure and hopefully we will have a new manager taking over so I can go back to being a player, even if Palace are relegated.'

Stepping back from the initial sensation that Lombardo was now in charge at Selhurst Park, the decision seemed to make sense. The players had apparently lost touch with Steve Coppell, necessitating a change, while the Italian international was the most senior member of the squad who would be guaranteed a first team place if fit. The only other candidate to fill the role would have been Andy Linighan, who might eventually be expected to forge a managerial career, but who had not featured in the starting line-up since the shambles at home to Wimbledon, thus taking him out of the running. What did not make sense was the ambiguous role handed to Tomas Brolin — a role misinterpreted by the press to such an extent that Palace's position as a national laughing stock was strengthened even further.

Officially, the Swede was given the charge of assisting Lombardo in translation from Italian to English. He was, after all, fluent following lengthy spells with Parma in *Serie A*. However, the media (in the latest mistranslation of Palace's increasingly linguistic season) pencilled Brolin in as Lombardo's assistant manager, a role he was never supposed to assume. Regardless of the Club's subsequent insistence to the contrary, Brolin remained Lombardo's Number Two in the press's eyes until relegation was confirmed in April. He took training sessions, issued advice from the dug-out and faced the television cameras just as an assistant manager would. The damage had been done.

Meanwhile, former Eagle Kenny Sansom arrived at Mitcham that morning with the intention of taking Palace's training session. He was under the impression that he had a role stipulated by the Club as a coach, replacing Brian Sparrow who had apparently been dismissed. Five minutes later, Sansom was driving out of the training ground, threatening a variety of law suits, having enjoyed the shortest spell as a coach in the history of football. He later suggested that Mark Goldberg and Ron Noades must have had a disagreement about his rejoining the Club, where he had made his name in the late 1970s, hence his brief appearance on the scene. Bemused by these comings and goings, the players surveyed the scene from afar, praying for an end to this ghastly Friday the 13th.

What about Ron Noades? Remember him? Palace's outspoken Chairman who was still very much in financial control of the Club. Where was he while all this was going on? Well, fittingly in this bizarre turn of events, he was on holiday, soaking up the sun in Spain, no doubt a few miles away from El Tel along the Costa Brava. However, Sansom's appearance had stung Ron into action and he subsequently explained his withdrawal from the public eye to Palace *Clubcall*.

'Recently I felt that it was better that I said nothing, particularly with the takeover potentially going through,' he explained. 'However, while I was away on holiday, some amazing things occurred at the Club. One or two other things, perhaps even more amazing, I managed to prevent from happening. Being a long way away at the time, I was opening my newspaper and reading the same stories that most Palace fans were reading. We were being linked with either Terry Venables, Ally McCoist, John Barnes and even Andy Goram. The constant links were unsettling the staff, as well as putting off the squad, coaches and even youth team players who were thinking of joining us for their apprenticeship. I think I have now managed to put an end to all those speculation stories and one or two people perhaps better understand the football business. The lessons learned will only stand those concerned in good stead for the future.'

This did nothing to suggest that the Club was united and benefiting from strong leadership from the top. He continued: 'While I was away, I received a phone call from Steve Coppell late on Thursday night saying that he wished to be relieved of his duties. He felt that we would certainly be relegated if he continued as manager, and that the players were not responding to him as well as they had been earlier in the season. He recommended that Attilio Lombardo took over. In my absence, Steve's suggestion seemed suitable.

'I went along with it, but found out the next day that we had apparently appointed Tomas Brolin as assistant manager, Kenny Sansom as a coach and asked Brian Sparrow to leave, none of which I had agreed to. By Friday lunch time, I had blocked the Sansom move and re-appointed Brian as I had not been consulted on either matter. Furthermore, I was assured that Tomas was merely assisting with translation for Attilio. There is only one assistant manager here and he is Ray Lewington, who is unfortunately still in hospital suffering from his knee injury.'

Big Ron was back, but some might argue that he should have been there to oversee such monumental upheavals all the time, although it is likely that the newspapers would have concentrated on Brolin's role whatever Noades had stated, for the Swede had become a figure of ridicule ever since his ill-fated spell at Elland Road. The true backlash against Graham Taylor's 1992 tormentor would not be felt until relegation had been sealed the following month.

At Villa Park on 14 March, Lombardo's first game in charge, Palace were lamentable before the interval. A concession after 56 seconds had practically handed John Gregory's side the points, and even Savo Milosevic scored twice to put the home side 3-0 up at the break. Palace seemed to be making a habit of allowing previously non-prolific strikers the opportunity to boost their goal tally, and the Yugoslav gratefully accepted the gifts handed to him on a plate. Matt Jansen's superb reply was nothing more than a consolation, but the travelling supporters cheered themselves up with a celebratory, carnival-like performance — anything to keep their minds off events on the pitch. On the final whistle, Attilio shrugged his shoulders and applauded his side's support. 'What more could I do?' he asked as other members of the team scuttled away without the smallest show of appreciation towards the banks of red and blue.

The Sunday papers had a field day. Frank McGhee, in *The Observer*, summed up the hopeless nature of Palace's plight: 'With a new non-English-speaking player-manager in Attilio Lombardo and a Swede in Tomas Brolin as his interpreter and assistant, Crystal Palace should be re-christened Tower of Babel. There certainly seemed to be few lines or signs of players communicating with each other very often during a defeat that anchors them even more firmly at the bottom. ... They look absolute certainties for the drop and it will take more than a Venables, even at his cutest, to produce any sort of revival.'

Paul Romain reflected upon an unhappy period in the match day programme for Palace's game with Spurs later in the month. 'The weekend defeat was possibly one of the lowest points I can recall since I started supporting the club in 1969,' he wrote. 'I can cope with defeats and constantly having to face hope turning to disappointment and dejection. I am, after all, a Palace fan and if I'm not used to it by now I might as well stop coming. ... What I could never stand is people laughing at Palace and actually having a point, and last week, with Attilio's elevation, the unofficial interpreter role for Tomas Brolin and the subsequent lampooning we received in the Sunday papers over the team talk that supposedly got lost in translation, we had just about crossed that boundary.'

The Club, for its part, stood up for the sudden change in management. Goldberg, who was finding the press slightly less of a friend than he might first have hoped, insisted that all the significant characters involved in the Selhurst soap opera were behind the move. 'Steve Coppell was happy to accept the new position and, as a fan of Crystal Palace, he supported the appointment of Attilio Lombardo,' he stated. 'The media may have ridiculed the move because it was convenient to do so — as it was to confuse the role of Tomas Brolin, whose extra responsibility it is to help communicate instructions out on the pitch — but those within the Club recognise the amount of respect that Attilio has at Selhurst Park. It was not logical to bring an outsider in at this stage. There wouldn't have been time for any new person to integrate and effect any change, so the appointment had to go to somebody already within the Club. Attilio is a very intelligent man and, with his respect and knowledge, he was the obvious choice.'

The manager, meanwhile, was disappointed at the excessive criticism his elevation attracted: 'I have been surprised by the cowardly remarks of the media. They poke fun at me, Tomas Brolin and, it seems, everyone else connected with the Club, but who is to say my appointment will prove a bad decision? Some people might say I can only improve on what has gone before.'

To this effect, the superb 2-1 victory at St James' Park which followed four days later pointed two fingers at the Club's detractors. Brave managerial decisions had been made, such as relying on a young strikeforce in Jansen and Marcus Bent against the Geordies, and the Eagles had come out on top. True, Newcastle were down in the dumps following comments allegedly made in a Spanish brothel by two directors who had subsequently refused to resign. True, Newcastle were struggling near the bottom of the table and had pinned all their hopes on the FA Cup to console their poor league form. In saying that, so had we!

True to form, the hacks concentrated rather more on Newcastle's failings than Palace's excellent performance. David Lacey in *The Guardian* pointed out that 'Newcastle lost at home to Crystal Palace, who had suffered eight successive league defeats and were still coming to terms with being managed by an Italian translated into English by a Swede.' To coin a footballing phrase, lads, give credit where credit's due. These were three well-earned points in the bag, rub of the green, game of two halves etc, etc. For one tantalising week, hope was rekindled among those of us naive enough to believe 'Popeye', as the Bald One had been christened, could perform the great escape. A win at home to fellow strugglers 'Spurs would drag heads above water, and the deadline day capture of Sasa Curcic from Aston Villa, after months of painful negotiation with the Birmingham club and the Department of Employment, added to the sense of anticipation.

Of course, it wasn't to be. Palace played spiritedly for the first hour against Christian Gross' side, with Sasa Curcic and Lombardo causing Ramon Vega and Colin Calderwood problems, with their willingness to run at the visitors' rearguard. Jansen, too, confirmed his immense promise with another skilful display, until he was dumped rather unceremoniously near the touchline and damaged his ankle in the process. All the optimism evaporated when Nicola Berti scored the softest goal of a season full of soft goals to put Tottenham ahead. Watching the ball loop agonisingly past the static Kevin Miller has to rank as one of the most painful moments of the season, and the subsequent capitulation surprised no-one. At least Shipps was back on the goal trail with his late effort. While Padovano, Lombardo and Shipperley had all returned to full fitness, Paul Warhurst remained seated in the stands, the defence crying out for someone with his know-how and class. Frustratingly, he would be the last of the injured players to return to the fold, and even then the temptation remained to play him out of position. But that is another story.

On 30 March, Palace's first team squad travelled to Tonbridge to take on the Angels in a memorial match for Freda, wife of the Club's Publications Manager, Pete King. The game had been organised by Pete and attracted a capacity crowd to the Longmead Stadium, along with former Eagles Ian Wright, Mark Bright, Andy Roberts and Phil Barber — testament to both Freda's and Pete's efforts on behalf of Crystal Palace over the years. Gareth Southgate sent a signed England shirt, and Ron Noades and Steve

Coppell were each handed a warm reception by the supporters. The impression was very much that of a homely club, in touch with its fans and anxious to repay those whose support had been tested by the traumas of the preceding few months. As the Angels and Eagles pitted their wits against each other in a relaxed, enjoyable atmosphere, for one blissful night the Premiership struggle could be forgotten...

...except it couldn't. In a way, that 1-0 victory over the Doctor Martens League Southern Section side encapsulated all the frustrations of watching Palace in the Premiership. Brolin misplaced every single one of his passes — literally, a 100 per cent failure rate to find a player in a red and blue shirt — while he lumbered along in the midfield, the game passing him by; Michele Padovano scored a striker's goal, but did very little else; the defence looked shaky and nervous, even up against strikers from a team fully eight divisions below them in the footballing hierarchy; veteran Phil Barber, guesting for his former club, was the only player apparently able to cross the ball from the left; while only Lombardo and Curcic seemed capable of putting on the show the crowds had flocked to see. The second half saw the youth team replace their senior counterparts and the juniors impressed, at least suggesting the future was not as bleak as the present appeared.

One incident in the game stands out in particular. As Palace came under increasing pressure before half-time (increasing pressure? What was going on?), Kevin Miller tipped a fierce shot from former Eagle Steve Lovell around the post, conceding a corner in the process. Skipper Marc Edworthy, who increasingly seemed a lone defender amidst the carnage of the Palace rearguard, patrolled the near post and cast an eye around the penalty area to check all were prepared to repel the cross. Spotting Italian Patrizio Billio standing idly outside the area — no doubt checking his hair in a conveniently sized pocket mirror — with two Tonbridge players totally unmarked in the box, Edworthy screamed out to the midfielder; 'Oi, Patrizio! Mark up! Mark up!'

Billio, disturbed from his day dreaming, looked up at the call of his name, puzzled by the confusion in the six yard box. 'Heh?' came the reply.

Football, the original universal language, claims another victim.

8 - April

GOODBYE AND GOOD RIDDANCE
The Sun, Tuesday, 28 April, 1998

In need of inspiration after the Tottenham and Tonbridge performances, Lombardo took his squad to the Desenzano boot camp near Lake Garda for training 'Italian style' and a spot of sight-seeing. Whatever tips and pointers he gleaned from the exercise would need to be implemented immediately if Palace was to avoid becoming the first club ever to fail to win a home league game throughout an entire season. It seemed their best chance of steering clear of such indignity would be against Leicester City over the Easter weekend. After all, the Foxes had barely mustered a whimper to prevent Bruce Dyer notching a hat-trick at Selhurst in January. In contrast, the rest of the month looked grim with Liverpool, Derby County and Manchester United on the agenda and all with plenty still to play for. Increasingly, it looked like victory or history against Martin O'Neill & Co on 11 April.

Given the extra onus on the Leicester fixture, the latest Selhurst 'please score three' hand-out could probably have been slightly better timed. Emile Heskey and Matt Elliott had decided to try on this occasion and scored the goals between them. Whatever Palace had worked on in Northern Italy, it clearly had not been basic defensive duties. At least Paul Warhurst returned after months on the sidelines, if only to be asked to lead the line rather than shore up the more than leaky defence. He subsequently reverted to the sweeper role at Anfield, but David Thompson's late winner there had such an air of inevitability about it that most took heart from only a 2-1 defeat.

The performance at Anfield was admirable in the circumstances. Having conceded mid-way through the first half, Palace for once harried their opponents, closing down the Merseysiders' flair players and rendering England's Steve McManaman a mere spectator. Even Tomas Brolin bit into tackles with a vengeance in the Palace midfield — perhaps he thought they were cream buns. Marcus Bent's lob (intended or otherwise) was utterly deserved and sent the marvellous travelling support into raptures. Bent, a Liverpool fan born and bred in London, emulated Jansen (at Newcastle) in scoring at his spiritual home and was beginning to show the form which would endear him to Eagles' fans over the final weeks of the campaign. The goal came after a period of frenzied pressure on the home defence and was only the fourth time all season to date that Palace had come from behind to equalise in the Premiership. Unfortunately, Liverpool upped a gear and, relentlessly attacking the Kop end, conjured a winner. The visitors deserved more, but left with nothing.

So another two games had floated down the pan without a point in sight. As if in response to the impending doom, the boardroom decided in its wisdom that it was time to re-enter the fray in the national press. With the takeover front relatively quiet, this month's specialist subject was 'team selection - the life and times of Attilio Lombardo'. With two minutes on the clock, it was the turn of Chairman Ron Noades to take centre stage.

'Contrary to popular opinion, I do not interfere with team selection,' he told *Clubcall*. He'd started so he'd finish. 'In saying that, I could not believe the side that was put out against Leicester. We seemed to put an emphasis on our trip to Anfield rather than the Leicester match, which is totally illogical. I would have thought that we would have been trying to win the Leicester match and prepared to forego the Liverpool game.'

Ron's comment was, in fact, a natural progression from his article in the match day magazine for the Leicester City fixture. Then, having already re-asserted his Chairmanship over the Sansom/Gascoigne fiascos, he had attacked his manager's line-up for the crucial London derby with 'Spurs. 'I was a bit disappointed that the side who played against Tottenham was not the same team that had beaten Newcastle,' he sighed. 'When I left Streete Court on Friday morning, the team on the training ground looked our strongest. In the event, perhaps a few of our side would have been better suited to positions on the bench as some of them were clearly not going to be able to play ninety minutes. In a way, I felt that we helped Tottenham Hotspur a bit with our team selection.'

Ron undoubtedly had a point, but perhaps should not have made his views public. It was just the latest nail in Palace's 'laughing stock' coffin and further ridiculed the decision to appoint Lombardo in the first place — a choice accepted by the Chairman at the time, albeit from a Spanish villa rather than his office at Selhurst Park. Warhurst's inclusion as a striker against Leicester was highly questionable, particularly when Jansen and Shipperley were rested from the squad purely with the trip to Liverpool in mind. The side selected against the Foxes would hardly have caused pangs of apprehension to pervade the visitors' changing room prior to kick-off, and the scratch team was duly annihilated. Similarly, Sasa Curcic's relegation to the substitutes' bench after an impressive display against 'Spurs was equally questionable.

'Loth as I am to criticise a man doing a sterling job that he didn't really ask for,' stressed Paul Romain, 'I have to say I'm not sure we are in a position to play the sort of squad game that United and Chelsea do regularly — we just don't have enough top quality players for the manager to be leaving himself or Sasa out at this level. One wonders whether we may now have a little more than a mere glimmer of hope if Sasa had started against

Leicester or Liverpool — the latter looked terrified of him running at them when he made an appearance late on. We shall never know!'

Attilio was upset by his Chairman's comments. He had not asked to be elevated into a role he clearly did not enjoy and, with the media flack already taking its toll, Noades voicing his opinion on matters close to home came as something of a stab in the back. As it was, the Italian stuck to his guns and relegated himself to the substitutes' bench for Derby County's visit.

18 April, 1998. Crystal Palace v Derby County.

Memories of a home victory to savour at last...

70 mins: after much huffing and puffing, Padovano is replaced by his compatriot and manager who is greeted with a rapturous reception by the crowd of just over 18,000, the majority of whom are simply basking in the reality that Palace have not, as yet, conceded three goals.

Witheroe: 'In a way, the Derby game reminded me of travelling up to Birmingham for the Liverpool semi-final. Absolutely no-one there gave us a chance of winning. We had gone out the week before against Leicester thinking we would win at home at last — they'd been rubbish in January in the Cup — but in the end the players almost seemed to have accepted that we were never going to win a league match at Selhurst. With Derby, though, it was different. We could remember the rearguard action we had had to perform up at Pride Park in December and, although Derby's form at the end of the season was poor, no Palace fan in their heart of hearts genuinely thought we would win the game.'

73 mins: Sasa Curcic performs an awesome piece of skill on the left flank to lose his marker and sends over a tantalising cross towards Neil Shipperley. Shipps, who had been playing as possibly the slowest right winger in history prior to his manager's arrival, cushions his header back across the edge of the area where Matt Jansen darts in and side-foots past Mart Poom. 1-0. The Holmesdale goes wild.

Wags: 'There was such comedy value attached to the whole game. There were people, myself included, who actually wanted us to go a whole season without winning a game at home at that stage, just purely to claim the record. We were expected to beat Sheffield Wednesday on the last day, but if we'd lost to Derby you would have to have bet against that happening!'

80 mins: Lombardo tears downfield having dispossessed Lars Bohinen on the edge of the Palace area, directing Curcic and Shipperley around him as the Derby defence back-pedals desperately. The Italian's perfectly weighted through ball finds the peroxide-stained Yugoslav who slots home past Poom at the near post. 2-0. Grown men start crying and the goalscorer is mobbed by a section of the Holmesdale. Meanwhile, two bemused Italian tourists seated in Block C renounce their AS Roma and Lazio allegiances on the spot, swept along by the emotion of a home win. You could see them asking each other, 'Surely this happens every week, no?' Not a chance, *mi amori*!

Ellis: 'It was great. By then, we all knew we were down, but we were just desperate to win a game. It was such an amazing party atmosphere, and seeing new players like Curcic obviously caring for the Club meant a lot to the fans. The whole day was superb.'

85 mins: Kevin Miller is hopelessly out of position after a Derby corner and Bohinen smashes the loose ball home. 2-1. More grown men begin to weep, while others renounce their faith on the spot.

Curcic: 'I want to dedicate this to all my friends, to Noades the chairman, to Goldberg, to everybody who gave me the last chance in my football life. I can never repay them for what they have done for me because a month ago I thought my football career was over. I was getting ready to go back to Yugoslavia. You cannot imagine how I have been feeling and today I have exploded with emotion.'

88 mins: Jonathan Hunt is allowed the freedom of SE25 to tear forward and unleash a 25 yard effort which clips the cross bar. Hearts stop beating. God is once again a Palace fan. Why does the referee insist on playing a full ninety minutes?

Witheroe: 'It was an absolutely storming end to the game. You'd be hard pressed to find a better ten minutes of football from last season. When they scored and then hit the bar... well, for entertainment value, it was superb stuff.'

89 mins: Bohinen lets fly again and is only denied by Miller's magnificent save, tipping the shot over the bar. Blow your whistle! People can barely watch as the visitors continue to pile on the pressure in search of the inevitable equaliser. If Derby score now... it's unthinkable. Why is life so cruel?

Wags: 'There were Derby fans in the pubs after the game who were totally humiliated. They'd only lost one game! The whole thing of losing to Palace was just too much for them to take. They'd lost at Selhurst, though, and that was a tag no-one had wanted to claim from the very first game of the season.'

90 mins: Lombardo (illegally?) robs Chris Powell and sets up Marcus Bent for the decisive third. Ecstasy. The Holmesdale is in danger of bouncing out of the ground and off towards central Croydon, while the deafening noise shatters windows in the corporate boxes as the champagne corks start popping. The scoreboard clicks in with, 'PALACE 3 DERBY 1. CHECK IT OUT!', while the Palace players collapse upon each other in a mixture of joy and relief. It is as if none of them has ever won a match at home in their lives. Nine of the thirteen on show that day had not done so in Palace colours. The crowds flock out of the stadium on the crest of a wave. First Selhurst, then the world.

Gordon: 'It's just a shame it didn't come ten home games ago.' Fair point, Deano.

Perhaps worried that Palace might still survive without him, Terry Venables chose the next day to reveal in his column in a tabloid newspaper that he would be in charge of the Eagles next season. He had apparently turned down offers to manage clubs in Greece, Spain and Germany in favour of a return to his roots, won over as he had been by Mark Goldberg's infectious enthusiasm. The salary was allegedly £600,000 per annum, although the chance to restore Palace to their rightful place amongst the élite was to be the new boss's chief motivation.

The news of Venables' imminent arrival was not unexpected as Goldberg had made it clear from the start that the former England coach was his number one choice to oversee the 'five-year plan' to European glory. As such, it was not 'new news'. However, it did provoke Palace's owner to put the appointment into perspective.

'It would be better if the takeover took place before Mark announced his plans for Palace, rather than the other way round,' Noades told *Radio Five Live*. 'If Mark Goldberg takes over the Club then Terry is saying that he has signed a contract to become manager. The deal hasn't been done yet and is dependent on the selling of shares in the market place. Its completion is the only time I will be sure.'

On *Clubcall*, he was quick to stress that Venables would not be winging in to Selhurst if the Goldberg deal was not finalised by the revised deadline. 'I believe that Venables is the best coach in the country, but, in my view, Crystal Palace could not afford the sort of salary that he would require. It may be that the hype involved in Terry coming here — which is what Mark is interested in — might justify the salary. He may indeed be able to do things for the Club that other people cannot achieve... However, to take on Venables would be a chance as, in my knowledge of the Club's finances, we could not afford him.'

Meanwhile, to ensure that his dreams would indeed be realised, the Chairman-Elect (who had shrunk away from the limelight somewhat since the passing of the transfer deadline) was said to have placed 2.5 million shares in MSB International PLC with institutional investors in an effort to raise some £23 million towards his acquisition of the Club. It appeared that the entire takeover would rely upon Goldberg being able to market the shares in time for the first instalment down-payment date. All the talk of stocks, shares and loan notes added to the impression that football was a mere aside to the complex business dealings of life in the Premiership. In a way, it was.

In fact, Goldberg sold at £10 a share, incidentally valuing MSB at £180 million. In today's transient late '98 markets the shares are around £4. Not bad, Mark!

However, life in the Premiership for Crystal Palace was ended abruptly live on SKY Sports on 27 April as Manchester United won comfortably in the capital. While the Palace programme commemorated a glorious 5-0 thrashing of the Red Devils back in December, 1972, the class of '98 only broke into something resembling a sweat when they realised they had not scored a third goal with seven minutes remaining. Andy Cole ensured they did not leave embarrassed. After all, they could hardly have claimed to be title contenders if they could not even win 3-0 at Selhurst Park, could they?

In truth, England's Paul Scholes, Nicky Butt and David Beckham must have relished the chance to face the tough-tackling, no-frills midfield of Brolin, Curcic and Lombardo. With Bent, Shipperley and Padovano also starting, the nearest Palace came to a 'holding player' in midfield was the portly Brolin, whose career in English football died a sad, pitiful death that night. Palace were relegated, but the fans had anticipated that well before kick-off. It was galling to watch United stroll to victory, but at least they weren't Brighton. Lombardo braved the television cameras after the game; 'We tried. No-one can tell us we didn't.' Few, however, had prepared themselves for the latest media backlash against the Club which exploded in the papers the following morning.

The headlines said it all; 'United afloat as Palace sink' (*The Guardian*), 'Down 'n out... Crystal Bawl, Palace shame as Scholes and Cole send 'em crashing!' (*The Sun*). The team selection, the abysmal home form, a defence devoid of all confidence and communication, a toothless attack and, above all, the off-the-pitch niggling and general chaos were all castigated by Fleet Street as no-one escaped unscathed. The chief target of the abuse would have found it hardest of all to hide.

'Now let us talk about Tomas Brolin,' said *The Sun*. 'It is incredible that he is playing in the Premiership. You have heard the phrase "He didn't cross the half-way line". Well Brolin did not even move off it. He is overweight, unfit, can't run, doesn't tackle. It took 68 minutes to take him off. He should never have started.' A similar attack was launched in the *Evening Standard*.

Brolin had arrived at the Club in January as a player hoping to prove himself at the highest level once again. He was an international star, the inspiration behind Sweden's exploits on the world stage in 1992 and 1994, but a flawed genius after an unhappy spell at Leeds United. Overnight, he had been branded a £4 million flop whom Leeds were only too glad to see the back of. Available on a free transfer, Steve Coppell had gambled and asked him to undergo a trial at the Club and, after realising that videos of the earth swallowing up Graham Taylor would not earn him a playing contract any more, Tomas had agreed. A week later, he found himself in the starting line-up against Everton as the Club's striking crisis forced Coppell's hand.

In his first two games for the Club, Brolin was fantastic. He struck the woodwork against Everton and, at Oakwell, had a goal disallowed against the Tykes and looked as distraught as any when both encounters ended in defeat. 'I have got my appetite back,' he told the press, although few needed to be reminded of that. His early enthusiasm earned him a contract until the end of the season and, at that stage, he looked worth his weight in gold (*ie:* a lot of money), especially once regular training began to work on his ample waistline.

Unfortunately for all concerned, the move did not work out quite as had been planned. A bruising encounter with Lucas Radebe in the opening exchanges of the 'grudge match' with Leeds appeared to sap his confidence. Constantly jeered by the travelling support from West Yorkshire and, with the abuse ringing in his ears, he faded into another dismal Palace home performance just when a player of his calibre should have stood up and inspired his team-mates. Indeed, the loudest cheer of that afternoon came when the ball cannoned onto the Swede's head in front of the away support, causing the bandage hastily applied after the earlier injury to explode dramatically into two pieces. Brolin's career appeared to self-destruct with it. In the press conference after the game, the visiting manager George Graham was asked whether he thought the Swedish striker was fit. 'I don't know,' he replied. 'I've never seen him fit.'

'He didn't seem to be up for it after that, and it all went downhill from then on in,' mused Neil Witheroe. Rare glimpses of the old Brolin could be seen if one really paid attention — a rasping drive from 30 yards against Derby, a glorious cross-field pass at Anfield — but the Club was not paying in excess of £8,000 a week for an ex-world beater. Off the field he conducted himself professionally and was always willing to talk to the media. He appeared to relish the role handed to him by Lombardo's appointment, whether that role had been misinterpreted or not, but his fitness had never improved. The Swede now markets sports shoes and he recently stated in a Swedish magazine that the experiences of last season taught him that he could no longer hope to perform in top division football. It was a sad end to an undoubtedly talented footballer's career.

The fact that Palace had chosen to rely on Brolin in their bid to escape the drop had further damaged the team's standing in the eyes of the footballing nation. The press's ceaseless attacks on the running of the South London Club ensured that there was little sympathy for the side when relegation was confirmed. 'And so we say goodbye to dear old Palace ("so the Eagle has landed - on it's backside"). Goodbye and good riddance. This once warm, friendly, family club go down with no sympathy' (*The Sun*). In the meantime, and in stark contrast, Barnsley remained the Premiership darlings whose 'brave, plucky' performances alone merited survival among the élite.

The constant references to the Tykes' battling team spirit became increasingly demoralising and frankly irritating. Here was a side who had finished fully nine points ahead of Palace in the 1996/97 season; had spent similar amounts of money pre-season on numerous foreign stars, many of whom had subsequently failed to make an impact; whose 'star' Macedonian striker had accused all women in Barnsley of being ugly in the national press, and whose disciplinary record was, quite simply, appalling. When three Barnsley players were dismissed at Oakwell against Liverpool, prompting a violent pitch invasion from a number of loveable home fans, the press continued to insist that Danny Wilson's players were simply 'battling hard to retain their Premiership status'. Battling, yes, but this was surely taking it a little too literally.

Everyone seemed to love Barnsley's attacking 'it's just like watching Brazil' style, which had resulted in them being hammered 6-0 at home to Chelsea, 7-0 at Old Trafford, 6-0 again at West Ham, 5-0 at Arsenal and by four goals against Wimbledon, Southampton and Everton. However, as soon as Palace attempted to employ gung-ho tactics, as Lombardo had attempted, they were shot down as unworthy of their Premier League place. The hypocrisy was astounding.

Of course, everyone loved Barnsley because they had never previously graced the élite and were seen as a small club breaking into a high-powered, rich man's world. They unearthed celebrity supporters who typified the gritty nature they hoped would keep them up. Harold 'Dickie' Bird's inarticulate mutterings would surely inspire Wilson & Co to greatness, and they were willing to 'give it a go'. Arguably, if Palace had not become embroiled in backroom squabbles, they too could have called upon some spirit of the underdog. But they had and, ultimately, even the Tykes' status as the nation's favourites was not enough to keep them in the Premier League. Who says romance is dead?

So Palace were down and out, disgraced and ridiculed by press and public alike. What better, then, in this slapstick season than to end the month by replacing the manager with a Chairman who was on the verge of selling the Club? No April fool... after all, this is Palace. Ron Noades, coaching badge warming his inside pocket, assumed control of team affairs at Selhurst Park on 29 April after Lombardo stepped down from his temporary position as player/coach. 'I'm looking after the football side until the end of the season,' Chairman, sorry 'manager' Ron told the media. 'Lombardo has decided that he wants to play only and not manage. He believes that is his strength and I'm inclined to agree with him.' The pantomime continued, although it was with open arms that Ray Lewington was welcomed back into the fold following his belated discharge from hospital.

Allegations flew that Lombardo had been dismissed and that he had found out the news on *Clubcall* or *Ceefax* (suddenly we were all wishing that Palace would feature a lot less on the television information service, which had become something of a portent of doom), suggestions quickly rebuked by the new man in charge: 'I find that quite laughable because Lombardo's had an interpreter here all year and so I can't believe he even listens to *Clubcall*.' It seems likely, however, that the Italian did feel diminished by his sudden relegation to the rank of mere player. It was no coincidence that speculation immediately surfaced regarding a switch to join forces with his old pal Vialli at Stamford Bridge, rumours which thankfully came to nothing.

Noades later reflected on his three games at the helm: 'It wasn't quite as reported in the papers. As Chairman, I've always had overall responsibility for everything that happens at the Club, whether it's football or not. Brian Sparrow, as coach, has been picking the side and Ray Lewington was fit enough to help him having returned after his operation. ... In terms of policy I make no apologies. I laid down the policy as to what we should be doing team-wise and I left it to my staff to implement that policy.' Brolin, Padovano and Billio were all conspicuous by their absence from the remaining games of the season.

While Palace's programme editor panicked over whose picture should adorn the manager's page of the match day magazine throughout May, the Eagles' players arrived at training with a sense of acute trepidation. As their third manager of the season prepared to put them through their paces, one unnamed player was quoted in the newspapers as saying 'Oh my God, this is the last thing we need. I suppose we shouldn't be surprised by anything that happens at this club. I really can't believe the Chairman is going to be selecting a Premiership team. I suppose he'll be travelling on the team bus as well.' Actually, he was probably driving it...

9 - May & June

THANK GOD IT'S ALL OVER
Rob Ellis, June 1998

In the early hours of 10 June, 1998, Mark Goldberg completed his £22m takeover of Crystal Palace Football Club from Ron Noades. The new Chairman wasted no time in appointing former Palace and England manager Terry Venables as the Eagles' new head coach, to work alongside Ray Lewington. By 10.00am, Noades had cleared his desk at Selhurst Park and the new regime had begun the arduous task of moving in. A significant day indeed.

You would have thought so, anyway. Instead, at a time when the nation was psyching itself up to support an England team devoid of Gazza in France '98, the news issuing from South London was largely ignored. After all, the takeover had been 'nearing completion' for an eternity, having already been delayed three months beyond the original February deadline. There were no elaborate frills or wildly sensational stories connected to the deal any more, not even a formal Selhurst Park press conference to announce to the world that Goldberg had taken over. (Venables was out of the country at the time of the completion, preparing to maintain his self-dignity on ITV's World Cup coverage; if he could do that, he could do anything). Instead, a simple press statement ending months of stalemate and frustration spluttered its way, almost apologetically, into Fleet Street's offices, making the news public. It was almost a masterpiece of anticlimax.

In a way, the month which elapsed after the end of the season was the most infuriating of all for Palace fans. May's three Premiership fixtures had seen fourteen goals, two sendings off and a carnival atmosphere wherever Palace played. Indeed, the four points gleaned from the Club's final three games in the Premier League represented a better haul than that accrued from the New Year until mid-April, such had been the extent of the Eagles' descent. Ron Noades, the manager, could afford to pat himself on the back. At the Reebok Stadium, his charges scored two of the best goals seen over the 1997/98 season, of which Dean Gordon's earned a nomination in *Match of the Day's* 'Goal of the Season', won unsurprisingly, if justifiably, by Dennis Bergkamp. Unfortunately, Bolton insisted on scoring five. Marcus Bent's effort in that game perhaps deserved a similar, if not greater accolade, but Bent surpassed himself once more with a delightful lob over Bernard Lama in the penultimate home game of the campaign — an entertaining 3-3 draw with ten-man West Ham United. Even in that game the players deemed that the supporters had not yet been through enough and kept us on our toes by conceding two late goals to a 19-year-old substitute, who had never previously scored in the first team and probably never would again. It hardly mattered.

Against Sheffield Wednesday, as Wags had predicted prior to the Derby County fixture, Palace won the game in the last minute as Clinton Morrison prodded home with his first touch in senior football. Only at Palace. Inevitably, the match was played at exhibition pace, as if it was a pre- or rather post-season friendly. While the players went through the motions, however, the supporters revelled in the knowledge that the end was nigh. A conga wove its way around the Holmesdale, before being rudely interrupted by the Public Address system demanding fans return to their seats and sit obediently while the Club slipped meekly out of the Premiership. Regardless, the festive atmosphere was reciprocated by the travelling fans from South Yorkshire and, in the warm, May sunshine, Palace's players bade farewell to the Premier League and their supporters. Neil Shipperley hurled his shirt into the crowd, while Attilio Lombardo clapped the 18,000 present and thanked them for their unbelievable patience. The sense of celebration seems perverse in retrospect, but the relief was enormous.

'The overriding feeling was "Thank God it's all over"' reflected Rob Ellis on the scenes at Selhurst that Sunday afternoon. 'I don't think anybody wanted the season to go on any further. We were all just fed up with it. We accepted we were down and just wanted to get on with next season.'

So the season could now be forgotten and the future shaped to ensure such catastrophes would never occur again. The installation of a new regime was the first step towards banishing those painful memories, and it was widely expected that Goldberg and Venables would take up the reins immediately. How naive we were...

A month later and most of us had toppled from our seats having spent four weeks perched precariously on the edge awaiting the ever-imminent news from Selhurst Park. In the meantime, it had all proved too much for Carlo Nash — a young, talented goalkeeper who had already proved his worth in the first division, but a player out of contract and offered a chance to move to Stockport County on a free transfer. With whom was he to re-negotiate a deal at Crystal Palace? Ron Noades, who seemed set to depart? Mark Goldberg, who was still officially only a director? Terry Venables, who was struggling manfully to hold a conversation with Bob Wilson on air? Who? The former Clitheroe 'keeper admitted to feeling totally rudderless at the South London Club and, with a certain amount of regret, opted to move on. He became the sixth senior player to leave since the end of the season, with Tomas Brolin and Patrizio 'Heh?' Billio the other significant, if inevitable, departures.

Perhaps more worrying were the speculative stories concerning Matt Jansen and Lombardo, both of whom were linked with moves back into the Premiership. Jansen, who had become something of a Selhurst hero during his brief spell at the Club and was widely tipped as one of the best young strikers in the English game, was the subject of £3.5 million bids from Southampton and Aston Villa. The danger was that the Eagles would lose out while time-consuming decisions were made at the top and disenchantment spread among the players. Lombardo, meanwhile, was apparently set to sign a cut-price £500,000 deal with his great friend Gianluca Vialli at Chelsea — in the same week that the Blues lined up moves for Pierluigi Casiraghi, Brian Laudrup and Marcel Desailly. In contrast, Lombardo's switch seemed to be dwarfed by the prospective transfer and wage demands made by the other three Ken Bates' targets.

'Popeye' was back in Italy while the stories circulated, as was Michele Padovano, who had presumably tired of training with Palace's reserves and was now being linked with moves back to *Serie A* and *Serie B* clubs. Furthermore, with Goldberg working hard to raise the £22 million to purchase the Club while simultaneously appeasing Midland Bank, holders of Palace's massive transfer debt, the press naturally assumed that a mass exodus from Selhurst Park would be the only way to balance the books. Out would go Lombardo, Jansen, Padovano, Bent, Shipperley, Gordon, Marc Edworthy and Bruce Dyer, leaving what was left of Steve Kember's reserve side to carry the promotion torch during the 1998/99 campaign. The second string would apparently be supplemented by a number of Terry Venables' signings — brought into the Club even before the manager and the Chairman who would be paying their wages — as David Howells, Gary Mabbutt, Dean Austin and a number of Australian internationals were all linked with the Club. As long as no news was issued, wild rumours continued to spread, leaving fans and players alike unsettled, uncertain and unsatisfied about the future.

Still, progress was being made all the time on securing the takeover deal and, to ensure the £22 million move went through, Goldberg suddenly found himself aided by an unlikely ally. Ron Noades announced on 5 May that he had lent Mark Goldberg £6 million to speed the completion of the deal, including an option on the freehold of Selhurst Park to be met within the next five years. This virtually guaranteed that the takeover would soon take place as only Midland Bank stood in the Chairman-Elect's way towards fulfilling his childhood dream.

What, then, of Chairman Ron? Why had he appeared to change his mind once more and encourage Goldberg to buy him out of the Club he had salvaged, nurtured and built up over seventeen hard years? The short answer would be £28 million. Noades is a businessman who was being presented with the perfect financial package, an offer he really could not refuse. Also, it is likely that his frustration at Croydon Council's lack of enthusiasm to sanction the development of Selhurst Park finally swayed his decision. He had always maintained that, until Palace could play their football in a 40,000 all-seater stadium, they would only be gate-crashing the Premier League party, and never able to hold their own among the élite. With the local authority either stalling or only favouring relatively minor improvements, Ron had had enough. Goldberg had arrived on the scene and made public his desire to own the Club, perhaps placing less significance on the stadium redevelopment, and seemed prepared to risk his personal fortune to achieve his goal. Ron could not lose.

Besides, Goldberg had come across as a Palace fan, something Noades had not done during his time at the Club — a fact of which he was much aware. On this purely tribal level, supporters would inevitably favour 'one of their own' at the helm, regardless of how much work and money Noades had put into the Club over his lengthy spell there. Supporter frustration had never unduly worried him in the past but, with the Club having over-spent in the Premier League and in need of recouping its losses by cashing in on two or three of its 'star' players, his standing among the fans would have depreciated further.

In an intriguing interview with Jimmy Hill in *Match of the Day Magazine*, Noades made no secret of the attractions of the deal put before him: 'I didn't want to sell Palace, but it went for £22.8 million excluding the ground. That goes into my holding company's assets, but I've lent Goldberg £6 million and, because he couldn't afford to buy the freehold, I've given him an option on it. So, in the end, Goldberg only came up with enough money to buy the Club. I think it was a stupid deal for him to do.

'I started off looking to sell ten per cent or about £3 million to spend on players to stay in the Premier League. He [Goldberg] wet his knickers about buying the place, but he just kept on and on. As soon as he signed a contract to buy it for £30 million, he went straight down to Steve Coppell and told him that he didn't want him to be manager.'

The disasters of the 1997/98 campaign had also taken their toll on the former property tycoon. 'The most rewarding part [of football] is in the lower divisions, working with young players who want to make the grade. When you get into the Premiership, like Palace's spell last season, I suddenly felt "I'm not really enjoying this" because the players wanted fortunes and didn't really give a toss about the Club. I thought I was being used. That was the first time I'd ever been disappointed. In the lower divisions, they're getting a pittance, but they're doing their best. You're all in it together.'

Of his successor at the helm, however, Noades conceded his respect for Goldberg's passion and enthusiasm; 'Mark's a nice guy. He just wanted Palace and he's put everything he's got, everything he's worked for, into it. I did the same in '81 — everything I had went into it. He's done the same. I don't mind whether he buys the freehold or not. I've made the offer — he's got five years on the freehold option.'

To some degree, most Palace fans will miss Ron's outspoken ways. His impact on Palace was phenomenal, enabling a club which was financially crippled and deserted by many of its supporters (the drop in attendance figures was unprecedented in the early 1980s) to achieve three promotions, five trips to Wembley, a ZDS Cup win, a third place finish in the top flight and to develop two ends of the stadium despite frosty relations with the local Council — all since 1989. In a way, Ron's success made his job even harder as Palace's best ever team, that of 1990/91, was broken up as ambitious players sought to move on to more fertile pastures. Ron would no doubt cite his inability to increase the capacity of Selhurst Park as chief among the reasons for being unable to establish the Eagles in the Premier League, but supporters tend to look at clubs like Wimbledon, Southampton and Coventry City and question why they seem to prosper while Palace continues to yo-yo. So much more could have been achieved under Ron had the Eagles survived the 1992/93 relegation fight, or even the 1994/95 unfortunate ('this year I think we'll relegate four clubs, as long as the fourth is Crystal Palace') scenario, enabling them to benefit from inflated television rights rather than stumbling along blindly in the first division. All that is in the past.

Within five days of the takeover's completion, Noades moved to Griffin Park, Brentford as the Club's new owner and first team manager. With him, he enticed Ray Lewington and Brian Sparrow, along with Gary Hargreaves from Palace's much improved marketing department to become his Managing Director. Soon, the exodus of Eagles' stalwarts reached Biblical proportions as chief scout John Griffin, further members of the backroom team and promising ex-trainees Danny Boxall and Robert Quinn followed manager Ron to West London.

'I'm doing something I've never done. I've never been allowed to be a manager, have I? Brentford will allow me to be manager — they'll have anyone other than David Webb, won't they?!' Ron told Jimmy Hill, explaining his decision to follow up his brief spell at the managerial helm at Selhurst Park with a more permanent appointment. In Lewington, Noades had captured one of the best coaches in the country and, one suspects, a figure who will be sorely missed at Crystal Palace.

At the time of writing, Noades had recently claimed the 'Manager of the Month' award for August, steering the Bees to the top of the third division. Furthermore, Hounslow Council appear to be comfortably receptive to the construction of a new stadium to help shape the future of Brentford FC. With money in the bank and success on and off the pitch, Ron is enjoying himself.

What of Palace's future under Mark Goldberg? If the Chairman's fabled five-year plan is to be successful, the Eagles need to bounce back to the Premiership at the first attempt — a task Terry Venables might be expected to achieve with the squad of players under his command. The departures have continued; Dean Gordon ended months of speculation by signing for Middlesbrough for £900,000, well below the initial rumours of a

£3 million switch to the North East; while Marc Edworthy has, rather surprisingly, returned to the Premier League with Coventry City. Conversely, there have been new signings from around the world, adding to the international flavour now associated with Selhurst Park and, inevitably, to doubts over communication at the back.

'Someone made the point, I can't remember who it was now,' reflected Neil Witheroe, '"Lots of people want to become football chairmen. Mark Goldberg wanted to become *Crystal Palace* chairman." Let's see what he can do.'

The 1998/99 league season began with a tremendous sense of optimism, cultivated by the new Chairman and those appointed by him. Perhaps anything would seem rosy when compared to the depths charted last season, but there has been a refreshing air about Selhurst Park so far, further encouraged by the sudden new-found ability to win at home! Meanwhile, at the plush Streete Court training centre (where, ironically, Ron Noades continues to be based), Venables and his array of coaches, fitness trainers and interpreters endeavour to spur Palace back into the big time. The future does look bright, but one suspects that Messrs Goldberg and Venables might come up against similar problems as their predecessors if Palace do gain promotion in May 1999. Still, let's enjoy the good times while they last.

On 19 July, 1998, Crystal Palace entered European competition for the first time since the Anglo-Italian Cup clashes of the 1960s. Samsunspor of Turkey visited Selhurst Park for a second round Intertoto Cup-tie, to be played over two legs, which would lead to a place in the UEFA Cup once the season was underway. The Eagles' entry into the competition had never been certain until the passing of the 2 June deadline for applications, ending reported interest from West Ham and Leicester City in the competition. Even then, there had been talk of the Eagles pulling out, anxious not to jeopardise their early season chances by picking up injuries in search of unlikely European qualification. Confusion reigned, with no-one quite sure whether or not Palace were in or out until, rather belatedly, UEFA had confirmed the original application.

Just prior to kick-off, chaos descended around the stadium as the unexpectedly large crowd of over 11,000 saturated the turn-stiles, pushing the starting time back fifteen minutes to 3.15pm. While pandemonium spread around him, Ron Noades calmly took his seat in the main stand. Steve Coppell, Steve Kember and Peter Nicholas were all at the ground, hoping to enjoy some entertaining football in the pleasant summer sunshine. With the mildly irritated crowd in place, Marc Edworthy exchanged pennants with the Turkish captain before rejoining Attilio Lombardo, Neil Shipperley and Hermann Hreidarsson, all busy warming up Kevin Miller in the home goal. The encouraging cry of 'Eagles! Eagles!' echoed around the stadium as the referee prepared to blow his whistle.

It could have been a scene taken from twelve months earlier. Now, though, Noades was a mere 'interested spectator', conscious of the fact that he had initiated the Club's interest in the Intertoto competition. Coppell, meanwhile, was present as Technical Director of Football and not as team manager. First team coach Terry Venables, in need of recuperation after his brushes with Bob Wilson across the Channel, was absent, leaving Mark Goldberg to herald in the new era at Selhurst Park alone.

In a way, the Intertoto tie represented too much of a legacy of the 1997/98 season. It needed to be brushed under the carpet, forgotten or ignored so that a new start could be made. The new management had hardly had the opportunity to familiarise themselves with the players' names, let alone their style of play or favoured positions. Unfortunately, and typically, the legacy lived on. Palace lost at home, 2-0, with the Turks missing a penalty in pursuit of the third goal. The tie was an inappropriate way to welcome the new regime, and represented rather the death-throes of the disastrous Premiership campaign. New era, same old Palace maybe, but the nightmares of 1997/98 had been exorcised once and for all. Rather than the customary Dave Clarke Five's song blaring from the PA system as the players trudged from the sun-saturated field that summer's afternoon, perhaps a more fitting chorus would have been '*Glad it's over!*' Hopefully, it is.

'David Hopkin, looking to curl one!' — Rob Hawthorne, 27 May, 1997.

ABOVE: 'What have I done?' Paul Warhurst sees the light. BELOW: So do Steve Coppell and Ron Noades.

80

Attilio (also INSET) nets at Leeds, leaving one ex-Eagle decidedly unamused in the background.

ABOVE: 'Heh, Gianluca. You should have joined Palace – at least you'd get into the side.' Lombardo and Vialli share a joke. BELOW: Ron Noades surveys the building site which was gradually transformed into Palace's plush Streete Court Training Ground. Unfortunately, Premier ambitions off the pitch were never matched upon it.

ABOVE: Dougie Freedman claims the man-of-the-match award for his performance against Bury in the Coca Cola Cup the previous season. The bike came in handy as he jumped on it to join Wolves in October. BELOW: Club interpreter Dario Magri explains the intricacies of the English language to Bruce Dyer while Padovano waits his turn.

ABOVE: Itzik Zohar on the South London leg of his European tour. BELOW: Steve Coppell cannot bear to watch as 'that penalty' is saved. Palace v Southampton, 26 December, 1997.

ABOVE: Warhurst had given all the machines in the treatment room names by the time he was ready to return to the senior side in March. BELOW: Pressures mount on Steve Coppell as results go from bad to worse. Ray Lewington, nearest to the camera, would be the latest to be struck down with injury as January turned increasingly sour.

ABOVE: The new man in charge, flanked by his predecessor and trusty interpreter, contemplates the folly of it all. BELOW: 'Heh, this is how a Premiership footballer ties his shoe laces:' Patrizio desperately tries to look the part.

ABOVE: Rumours abounded that Brolin's number 12 shirt had been made by a tent company, designed to fit the Swede's rotund torso. BELOW: The end is nigh. Palace contemplate introducing Clinton Morrison against Sheffield Wednesday.

'I really can't believe the chairman is going to be selecting a Premiership team. I suppose he'll be travelling on the team bus as well.' Actually, he was probably driving it...

'Who are you calling big head?' Chairman Mark Goldberg tries on the new kit for size as his takeover is completed in June.

'Hmmm, I'm done with Crystal Palace. Let's have a go at Brentford.'

Appendix i
PALACE RESULTS 1997-1998

DATE	OPPONENTS	F-A		CROWD	SCORERS
Sat 9 Aug	Everton	W	2-1	35,716	Lombardo, Dyer (pen)
Tue 12 Aug	Barnsley	L	0-1	21,547	
Sat 23 Aug	Leeds U	W	2-0	29,076	Warhurst, Lombardo
Wed 27 Aug	Southampton	L	0-1	15,036	
Sat 30 Aug	Blackburn R	L	1-2	20,849	Dyer
Sat 13 Sept	Chelsea	L	0-3	26,186	
Tue 16 Sept	Hull (CCC2)	L	0-1	9,323	
Sat 20 Sept	Wimbledon	W	1-0	16,747	Lombardo
Wed 24 Sept	Coventry	D	1-1	15,900	Fullarton
Sat 27 Sept	Bolton W	D	2-2	17,134	Warhurst, Gordon
Tue 30 Sept	Hull (CCC2)	W	2-1	6,407	Veart, Ndah
Sat 4 Oct	Man Utd	L	0-2	55,143	
Sat 18 Oct	Arsenal	D	0-0	26,180	
Sat 25 Oct	Sheff Wed	W	3-1	22,072	Hreidarsson, Rodger, Shipperley
Sat 8 Nov	Aston Villa	D	1-1	21,097	Shipperley
Mon 24 Nov	Tottenham	W	1-0	25,634	Shipperley
Sat 29 Nov	Newcastle	L	1-2	26,085	Shipperley
Wed 3 Dec	West Ham	L	1-4	23,335	Shipperley
Sat 6 Dec	Leicester	D	1-1	19,191	Padovano
Sat 13 Dec	Liverpool	L	0-3	25,790	
Sat 20 Dec	Derby Co	D	0-0	26,590	
Fri 26 Dec	Blackburn R	D	2-2	23,872	Dyer, Warhurst
Sat 3 Jan	Scunthorpe (FAC3)	W	2-0	11,624	Emblen (2)
Sat 10 Jan	Everton	L	1-3	23,311	Dyer (pen)
Sat 17 Jan	Barnsley	L	0-1	17,819	
Sat 24 Jan	Leicester (FAC4)	W	3-0	15,489	Dyer (3)
Sat 31 Jan	Leeds U	L	0-2	25,248	
Mon 9 Feb	Wimbledon	L	0-3	14,410	
Sun 15 Feb	Arsenal (FAC5)	D	0-0	37,164	
Sat 21 Feb	Arsenal	L	0-1	38,094	
Wed 25 Feb	Arsenal (FAC5r)	L	1-2	15,674	Dyer
Sat 28 Feb	Coventry	L	0-3	21,810	
Wed 11 Mar	Chelsea	L	2-6	31,917	Hreidarsson, Bent
Sat 14 Mar	Aston Villa	L	1-3	33,781	Jansen
Wed 18 Mar	Newcastle	W	2-1	35,565	Lombardo, Jansen
Sat 28 Mar	Tottenham	L	1-3	26,116	Shipperley
Sat 11 Apr	Leicester	L	0-3	18,771	
Mon 13 Apr	Liverpool	L	1-2	43,007	Bent
Sat 18 Apr	Derby Co	W	3-1	18,101	Jansen, Curcic, Bent
Mon 27 Apr	Man Utd	L	0-3	26,180	
Sat 2 May	Bolton W	L	2-5	24,449	Gordon, Bent
Tue 5 May	West Ham	D	3-3	19,129	Bent, Rodger, Lombardo
Sun 10 May	Sheff Wed	W	1-0	16,878	Morrison

Appendix ii

FA CARLING PREMIERSHIP 1997/98

	P	Home					Away					PTS
		W	D	L	F	A	W	D	L	F	A	
Arsenal	38	15	2	2	43	10	8	7	4	25	23	78
Manchester United	38	13	4	2	42	9	10	4	5	31	17	77
Liverpool	38	13	2	4	42	16	5	9	5	26	26	65
Chelsea	38	13	2	4	37	14	7	1	11	34	29	63
Leeds United	38	9	5	5	31	21	8	3	8	26	25	59
Blackburn Rovers	38	11	4	4	40	26	5	6	8	17	26	58
Aston Villa	38	9	3	7	26	24	8	3	8	23	24	57
West Ham United	38	13	4	2	40	18	3	4	12	16	39	56
Derby County	38	12	3	4	33	18	4	4	11	19	31	55
Leicester City	38	6	10	3	21	15	7	4	8	30	26	53
Coventry City	38	8	9	2	26	17	4	7	8	20	27	52
Southampton	38	10	1	8	28	23	4	5	10	22	32	48
Newcastle United	38	8	5	6	22	20	3	6	10	13	24	44
Tottenham Hotspur	38	7	8	4	23	22	4	3	12	21	34	44
Wimbledon	38	5	6	8	18	25	5	8	6	16	21	44
Sheffield Wednesday	38	9	5	5	30	26	3	4	13	22	41	44
Everton	38	7	5	7	25	27	2	8	9	16	29	40
Bolton Wanderers	38	7	8	4	25	22	2	5	12	16	39	40
Barnsley	38	7	4	8	25	35	3	1	15	12	47	35
Crystal Palace	**38**	**2**	**5**	**12**	**15**	**39**	**6**	**4**	**9**	**22**	**32**	**33**

INDEX

All figures in *italics* refer to illustrations.

AC Milan 40,48
Adams, Micky 17
Adebola, Dele 31
AEK Athens 52
Al Fayed, Muhammed 17
Alexander, Phil 23
Amsalem, David 38
Andersen, Leif 29
Anfield 63,64,69
Anglo-Italian Cup 77
Armstrong, Chris 11
Arsenal ('The Gunners') 15,46,50,52,
 55,70
AS Roma 65
Aston Villa 28,48,55,61,74
Austin, Dean 74
Australian FA 52
Azzurri 14,25,41
Baggio, Roberto 13,14
Baker, Danny 48
Barber, Phil 61,62
Barnes, John 54,59
Barnet 31
Barnsley ('The Tykes') 24,29,45,70
Bassett, Dave 10,12,13,31,47
Bastia 15
Battega, Roberto 52
Bates, Ken 57,74
Beckham, David 68
Beitar Jerusalem 41
Bent, Marcus ... 47,49,61,63,66,68,72,74
Bergkamp, Dennis 18,29,30
Berkovic, Eyal 37,38,39,41
Berti, Nicola 61
Biggin Hill 18
Bilic, Slaven 19
Billio, Patrizio 31,62,71,73,*86*
Bird, Harold 70
Birmingham 49,61,65
Blackburn Rovers 15,17,25,40,42
Bohinen, Lars 65,66
Bolton Wanderers 12,16,19,24,25,29,
 31,37,72
Bolyn Ground 37
Bonetti, Ivano 31,57
Boothferry Park 25,26
Bosman (Ruling) 11,32,56
Boxall, Danny 76
Brazil, Alan 9,12
Brentford 47,76
Bright, Mark 61
Brighton & Hove Albion 68

Brolin, Tomas .. 28,46,58,59,60,62,63,68
 73, *87*
Brown, Craig 12
Burnden Park 12,31
Bury 24,*83*
Butt, Nicky 68
Calderwood, Colin 61
Cannes 52
Capital Gold 22
Carlisle United 47
Casiraghi, Pierluigi 74
Ceefax 10,11,70
Champions' League 47
Championship Manager 2 48
Charlton Bobby 14
Chelsea 15,24,25,26,27,39,55,70,74
Claridge, Steve 9,10
Clitheroe 73
Clubcall .. 13,14,20,22,34,48,58,64,67,70
Coca-Cola Cup 25,26,*83*
Cole, Andy 68
Collymore, Stan 13
Coppell, Steve .... 10 *passim, 80,84,85*
Corsica 14
Coventry City 37,46,48,53,76,77
Craven Cottage 4
Crazy Gang 55
Crewe Alexandra 33
Croydon 18,66
 Council 28,35,74
Cup Winners' Cup 24
Curcic, Sasa 48,49,61,62,64,65,66,68
Cyrus, Andy 12
Darby, Duane 25,26
Dave Clarke Five 78
Davies, Gareth 31
 Kevin 37
Dawes, George 14
Day, Chris 12,31
Dell, The 19,24,37
Department of Employment 61
Derby County .. 14,37,39,46,65,66,69,73
Desailly, Marcel 74
Desenzano 63
Di Matteo, Roberto 18,24
Dodd, Jason 38
Domark 29
Doncaster 25
Dublin, Dion 48,49
Dyer, Bruce 10,17,19,24,31,32,38,
 40,46,53,*83*
Eagle Eye 46
Eagles Magazine 23,50,51
Edworth, Marc ... 10,17,24,29,37,41,62,
 74,77

Elland Road 11,12,20,59
Elliott, Matt 15,63
Ellis, Rob 10,24,31,41,66,73
Emblen, Neil 19,24,41,42,45,50
Endsleigh League 31
Everton 19,45,46,70
Evening Standard 68
Ewood Park 43
Exeter City 12
FA Cup 43
Ferdinand, Les 13
Ferguson, Alex 29
  Duncan 19
FIFA 48
Filbert Street 37
Finland 13,38
Flo, Tore Andre 24
Football Italia 14
Francis, Gerry 51,57
Freedman, Dougie 10,31,32,33,*83*
Fry, Barry 49
Fulham 42
Fullarton, Jamie 15,19,21,25
Furlong, Paul 21
Gabbiadini, Marco 38
Gascoigne, Paul ('Gazza') ... 13,28,38,48,
                                     49,64,72
Geller, Uri 17
Genoa 14
Ginola, David 18
Ginty, Rory 43
Glasgow Celtic 15,48
  Rangers 52
Goldberg, Mark .... 15 *passim*, 89
Goodison Park 19,40
Goram, Andy 48,59
Gordon, Dean 9,10,66,72,74,76
Graham, George 11,12
Gray, Andy
  (former Palace player) 11
  Andy (SKY pundit) 21,29
Gregory, John 59
Greece 67
Green, Alan 22
Griffin, John 76
  Park 76
Grimsby 31
Gross, Christian 30,61
Guardian, The 61,68
Guillit, Ruud 18,23,24,55,57
Hargreaves, Gary 76
Harris, Jason 31
Hateley, Mark 25,26
Hawthorne, Rob 9,79
Heskey, Emil 63
Highbury 46
Highfield Road 25,48
Hill, Jimmy 75
Hillsborough 16,28,30
Hirst, David 37

Hoddle, Glenn 23
Hodgson, Roy 25
Holmesdale Stand 40,45,49,65,66,73
Hopkin, David 9,10,11,12,19,20,31,
                           38,45,46,79
Houghton, Ray 10,12,31
Hounslow Council 76
Howells, David 74
Hreidarsson, Hermann 19,22,29,30,
                                 41,55,77
Hughes, Mark 24
  Paul 24
Hull City ('The Tigers') 25,26,27,39
Hunt, Jonathan 66
IBV Knattspyrnurad 21
Iceland 21
IFK Gothernburg 28
Ince, Paul 13
Intertoto Cup 77,78
Ismael, Valérien 47,49
ITV 72
Izzet, Mustafa 37
Jansen, Matt ... 47,49,50,59,61,63,64,65,
                              73,74
Johnson, Tommy 48
Jones, Dave 37
  Paul 40
Juventus 26,28,29,33,35,42,52,54,57
Keegan, Kevin 17
Kember, Steve 34,40,74,77
Kendall, Howard 9,19
Ketsbaia, Temuri 39,48
Keys, Richard 29
King, Freda 61
  Pete 53,61
King's Road 55
Kop, The 64
Koswell, Leo 48
Lacey, David 61
Lake Garda 63
Lama, Bernard 72
Laudrup, Brian 74
Lazio 33,65
Laws, Brian 45
Le Saux, Graeme 24
Le Tissier, Matthew 38
Leaburn, Carl 46
Leboeuf, Frank 18,24
Leeds United ... 11,12,21,23,68,69,*80,82*
Leicester City ('The Foxes') 9,14,29,
                           42,46,55,63,64
Lewington, Ray ... 10,13,14,38,41,43,45,
                    47,49,55,57,59,70,71,72,76,*85*
Lewis, Joe 52
Leyton Orient 31
Lineker, Gary 29
Linighan, Andy 10,22,58
Little, Brian 57
Liverpool 19,37,38,42,49,63,65
Loftus Road 19

Lombardo, Attilio .... 13 *passim, 81,86*
Longmead Stadium 61
Lovell, Steve 62
Lucan, Lord 55
Luzardi, Luca 31
Lynam, Desmond 29
Mabbutt, Gary 74
Maccabi Haifa 40
    Tel Aviv 38
Mackrell, Graham 16
Magri, Dario 42,57,*83*
Manchester City 10,23,47
    United 39
    ('The Red Devils') 23,29,49,55,67
Martyn, Nigel 10,11,12
Match of the Day 29,57,72
    Magazine 75
McAteer, Jason 12
McCoist, Ally 59
McDonald, Trevor 48
McGhee, Frank 32,60
McGoldrick, Eddie 12
McKenzie, Leon 42
McManaman, Steve 63
Middlesbrough 23,33,48,76
Midland Bank 74
Mihailov, Bobby 16
Milan 18
Miller, Kevin ... 12,13,17,19,21,29,38,61,
                                  62,66
Millwall 16,17,31
Milosevic, Savo 59
Mitcham 12,38,42,49,52,56,58
Molineux 32,42
Morecambe 37
Morrison, Clinton 42,73,87
MSB International PLC 67
Muscat, Kevin 30
Nash, Carlo 21,73
Nationwide League 10,23,28,47,54
Ndah, George 26,31,49
Neville, Gary 32
Newcastle 26,38,39,52,61,63
News at Ten 48
Nicholas, Peter 10,77
Nicholls, Mark 24
Noades, Ron .... 10 *passim, 80,82,88,90*
Nottingham Forest 12,23
O'Neill, Martin 24
Oakley, Matthew 38
Oakwell 30
Observer, The 60
Old Trafford 28,29,32,39,70
One More Point 42,56
Oster, John 19
Oulu 38
Overmars, Marc 13,18
Owen, Michael 37
Oxford United 15
Padovano, Michele ... 28 *et seq*, 31,33,34,
      35,36,42,43,46,47,52,53,56,61,*83*

Palace Radio 22
Palmer, Carlton 37
Pearce, Jonathan 22,29
Petrescu, Dan 18
Pistone, Alessandro 13,42
Pitcher, Darren 20,43
Play-offs 9
Pleat, David 16,57
Poom, Mart 65
Powell, Chris 66
Preece, Andy 22
Premiership, FA Carling
    (Premier League) .... 9 *passim*
Pride Park 37
Quinn, Robert 76
Radebe, Lucas 69
Radio Five Live 22,67
Ravanelli, Fabrizzio 52
Reading 12,17,30
Real Betis 55
Redfearn, Neil 24,25
Reebok Stadium 72
Rennie, Uriah 37
Richardson, James 14
    Kevin 37
Roberts, Andy 10,16,17,29,30,39,43,
                              55,56,61
Robson, Bryan 33
Rodger, Simon 9,29,43,56
Romain, Paul 12,24,25,26,41,60,64
Rome 28,41
Root's Hall 31
Rosenthal, Ronny 38,39
Royal Antwerp 38
Russia 28
Sadler, Gary 41,42,43,46
Salako, John 12,48,49
Sampdoria 14,57
Samsunspor 77
Sansom, Kenny 58,64
St James' Park 42,60
Scholes, Paul 68
Scunthorpe United 43,45
Selhurst Park .... 10 *passim*
Selhurst Six 53
Serie A/B 28,52,54,74
Shaw, Richard 12
Sheffield United 9,10
    Wednesday 16,37,73,*87*
Shipperley, Neil ... 17,28,30,32,36,37,38,
            39,41,42,61,64,65,68,73,74,77,
Signori, Beppe 28,33
SKY television 12,17,22,29,46,67
Smith, Alan 31
    Jamie 32,36,41,43
Sogliano, Sean 31
Souness, Graeme 37
Southam, Neville 19
South Norwood (SE25) 10,16
Southampton ('The Saints') 24,37,38,
                         41,70,74,76,*84*

Southend United 31
Southgate, Gareth 61
Sparrow, Brian 55,59,71,76
Stamford Bridge ... 23,25,54,55,56,57,71
Stevenage Borough 31
Stockport County 37,73
Strachan, Gordon 53
Streete Court 47,55,64,77,*82*
Sugar, Alan 30
Sun, The 68
Sunderland 23
Swansea City 25
Swindon Town 30,32
Taberner House 34
Taylor, Gareth 38
     Graham 59,68
Tel Aviv 40
Telfer, Paul 53
Thomas, Geoff 12
Thompson, David 63
Tiler, Carl 9
Tonbridge Angels 61,63
Tottenham Hotspur ('Spurs') .. 29,30,51,
     54,63,64
Turin 16,18,33,35,43
Tutosport 52
Tuttle, David ('Tutts') 10,22,41
UEFA 49,55,77
Veart, Carl 26,31
Vega, Ramon 61
Venables, Terry ('El Tel') 48,51,52,54,
     55,56,57,59,67,72,73,76,77,78

Vialli, Gianluca 14,17,18,24,55,56,71,74
Villa Park 55,59,*82*
Vicarage Road 12
Wags (*One More Point*) 42,56,65,73
Warhurst, Paul 17,19,24,31,32,43,61,
     63,64,*80,85*
Watford 12
Webb, David 76
Wembley Stadium .... 10 *et seq,* 16,17,19,
     25,31
Wenger, Arsène 18,30
West Ham United 37,39,43,52,70,
     72,77
Whilmot, Rhys 20
White Hart Lane 29,30,33,43,51,56
Wilkins, Ray 17,22
Wilson, Bob 78
Danny 70
Wimbledon 30,41,46,55,58,70,76
Witheroe, Neil 46,48,50,65,66,68,77
Wolverhampton Wanderers 19,31,32
Wordsworth, Dean 31
World Cup 12
Wright, Ian
     (Crystal Palace & Arsenal) 11,61
     (Hull City) 26
Yorkshire 12
Young, Eric 31
Zenith Data Systems Cup 76
Zohar, Itzik .... 21,34,38 *et seq,* 46,*84*
Zola, Gianfranco 18,24,55,56
Zurich 30